DEPARTMENT OF ENGLISH LOCAL HISTORY

OCCASIONAL PAPERS

Edited by H. P. R. FINBERG

No. 18

The Deserted Villages of Northamptonshire

by

K. J. ALLISON,
M. W. BERESFORD, J. G. HURST
and other members of the
Deserted Medieval Village Research Group

LEICESTER UNIVERSITY PRESS
1966

Printed at The Broadwater Press
Welwyn Garden City, Herts
for the
Leicester University Press

PREFACE

LIKE its companion, *The Deserted Villages of Oxfordshire*, this reconnaissance has been achieved by the co-operation of several members of the Deserted Medieval Village Research Group. All the sites listed in the Gazetteer have been visited by the Secretary, Mr J. G. Hurst, who is responsible for the proposed identification of sites, the reports on their condition, and the notes on excavations. Through the good offices of the Vice-Chairman of the Group, Professor H. C. Darby, Mrs Betty Grant held a Research Fellowship at University College, London, for the purpose of working over the main Public Record Office documents concerning this and other Midland counties. The Gazetteer was written by Dr K. J. Allison, drawing upon Mrs Grant's notes and upon earlier work by Professor M. W. Beresford. Professor Beresford is responsible for the proposed dates for depopulations and for the text of the Introductory Essay. Dr R. E. Glasscock has prepared the distribution maps and also made available from his unpublished London Ph.D. thesis his identifications of vills in the 1334 Lay Subsidy. Mr Hurst and Professor Beresford have had access to the R.A.F. air photograph collection in the Library of the Ministry of Housing and Local Government, and to the Cambridge Air Photograph Collection in the curatorship of Dr J. K. S. St Joseph. Mr P. I. King has assisted with material from the Northamptonshire Record Office. Professor Beresford and Mr Hurst also thank Mr John Sheail and Mrs Wendy Gilding for assistance in preparing the manuscript and Mr J. Evans, Mr Alan Palmer, and Mr K. Gilbert for checking the text of the Gazetteer.

A grant towards publication has been made by the British Academy.

The Group and the authors wish to thank the General Editor of these *Occasional Papers*, Professor H. P. R. Finberg, for his sponsorship of these two county studies.

CONTENTS

THE DESERTED VILLAGES OF NORTHAMPTONSHIRE

INTRODUCTORY ESSAY

I

THIS introductory essay is complementary to that in a previous Occasional Paper, *The Deserted Villages of Oxfordshire*.[1] The material in the Gazetteer is also arranged similarly, using the same abbreviations, and the maps use the same conventional signs. Many of the Tables have the same form as in the Oxfordshire essay, and frequent comparisons between the experience of the two counties will be observed.

The two counties have a common boundary from near Brackley to the Three Shire Stones, which are near Wormleighton, a distance of twenty-one miles. Geologically, a small area in the south-west of Northamptonshire is akin to the Cotswolds proper, but the Northampton Heights, with their scarp facing the Avon valley, continue the spine of high ground from the Cotswolds as far as the edge of Rockingham Forest. Northamptonshire has its late-surviving forest areas in Whittlewood and Rockingham, and in the north-east there is an area of peat fenland between Welland and Nene which is unmatched in Oxfordshire.

With this internal variety it is to be expected that the intensity of depopulation is not the same in all parts of the county, but in its general experience Northamptonshire is unmistakably a Midland county, akin to the eight counties which border upon it: Oxfordshire, Warwickshire, Leicestershire, Rutland, Lincolnshire, Huntingdonshire, Bedfordshire, and Buckinghamshire. This recital of neighbouring counties does more than reiterate the Midland character of Northamptonshire, for it evokes the names of those counties most frequently on the lips of public men in the decades of the sixteenth century when the causes and consequences of depopulation were being most vigorously argued. Time and time again the words and actions of pamphleteers and legislators showed that to them depopulation was basically a Midland problem.[2]

Looking back from the early seventeenth century Richard Sandes advised Charles I's Privy Council that "depopulated towns (are) in the best naturall

---

[1] University of Leicester, Department of English Local History, *Occasional Paper* no. 17 (1965).

[2] M. W. Beresford, *The Lost Villages of England* (1954; 4th imp. with corrections, 1963), pp. 106–17 and 217–46; also 'Villages désertés: bilan de la recherche anglaise', in École Pratique des Hautes Études, VIe section, *Villages Désertés et Histoire Économique, XIe—XVIIIe siècle* (Paris, 1965), pp. 533–80 for a review of work since 1954; on the Midlands see also J. D. Gould, 'Mr Beresford and the Deserted Villages' in *Ag. Hist. Rev.*, III, 1955, pp. 107–13.

corne countryes which affore supplyed the wants of others every way, beinge in the middle of the land,"[1] and the author of one of the most often-quoted pamphlets of the mid-sixteenth century, *The Decaye of England only by the Great Multitude of Shepe*, had no doubts that the experience of Northamptonshire and Oxfordshire was all of a piece together. After asking rhetorically where the displaced husbandmen from the Oxfordshire villages should go for employment, he concluded: "These ... persons had need to have living: whither shall they go? into Northamptonshire? and there also is the living of persons lost."[2] The study of Oxfordshire has shown that not all the county's deserted sites can be attributed to the period of the devouring sheep: yet the proportion is probably as high as 40–50 per cent. How does Northamptonshire appear? In order to answer this question it is necessary to review the materials available for the identification of deserted sites and for the dating of their depopulation. The character of the documentary material and the small number of sites that have received any archaeological attention make it impossible to give firm dates for every depopulation, and the symbol N in the Gazetteer is an acknowledgement of the limits of the present state of knowledge. Further local investigation, however, should lighten the darkness, and the present reconnaissance conducted largely from London is intended to stimulate and assist local inquiries, even if the result is the qualification of its conclusions and the revision of its statistics.

II

For the majority of Northamptonshire villages, whether surviving or now deserted, the earliest documentary evidence is afforded by Domesday Book, compiled for William I in 1086. However, some villages have their bounds delineated in surviving charters from the Anglo-Saxon period, and among these are five that are now deserted: Fawsley and Snorscomb (with a charter of 944), Nunton (963), Churchfield (964), and Achurch (*c.* 980). In Domesday Book, apart from Northampton, 323 separate places are mentioned within the bounds of the present county,[3] and of these 38 are no longer to be found as settlements. Some have their names perpetuated in the names of modern farms, fields, and woods: others have no memorial. The five persons (perhaps heads of households) at *Calme* in 1086 and the nine at *Brime* may be said to be the whole recorded history of these places, and the sites can be located only approximately. For Northamptonshire there is available some evidence ancillary to Domesday Book through the Geld Roll (compiled before 1076) and

[1] Public Record Office (hereafter cited as P.R.O.) SP16/206/69.

[2] R. H. Tawney and E. E. Power, *Tudor Economic Documents*, 1937, III, pp. 52–3: "Our complaynt is for Oxford-shyre, Buckyngham-shyre and Northampton-shyre."

[3] H. C. Darby and I. B. Terrett (eds.), *The Domesday Geography of Midland England*, 1954, pp. 382–4.

the twelfth-century 'Northamptonshire Survey'. These documents say very little more about the size and character of settlements but they assist in the identification of some difficult Domesday place-names.

While places such as *Calme* and *Brime* were passing into oblivion there were other settlements coming into existence, particularly in those parts of the county that the distribution map of Domesday settlements shows as lightly settled in 1086, especially the forest and fen of the north-east. Thus twelve of the places that were later to be deserted have no documentary record earlier than the twelfth century, and another seventeen have not yet been noticed in documents of a date earlier than 1200.[1]

As Table III will show, Northamptonshire has a smaller proportion of early losses of settlement[2] than either Oxfordshire or Leicestershire, the counties whose general depopulation history it otherwise closely resembles. Between *c.* 1100 and *c.* 1350, when these two other counties lost 8 per cent of their deserted sites, Northamptonshire lost only a single site, Pipewell, with a recorded population of nine in Domesday Book. It is more than likely that the foundation of the Cistercian Abbey of Pipewell in 1143 caused the extinction of this village community. The site of the abbey was placed east of the village, and the village site was incorporated in the West Grange of the abbey. No other depopulation in Northamptonshire can be attributed to the Cistercians,[3] and since the four settlements which have no record beyond Domesday Book have yet to be traced on the ground it will clearly be some while before the silence of documents can be corrected by the spade and trowel of the archaeologists; even the site of West Grange, it will be noted, is not certainly identified.

III

Unfortunately Northamptonshire does not have the village surveys from the Hundred Rolls of 1279 which were so useful in charting the progress of settlement in Oxfordshire, and the first county-wide information about the distribution of settlement near the peak of medieval population (i.e. *c.* 1300) comes from the record of the tax paid by the laity in 1301.[4] From this, for example, we know that the village of Achurch, now deserted, then had 28 persons wealthy enough to engage the tax collectors' attention and each of these can be

---

[1] Using the evidence of documents scrutinized by J. E. B. Gover, A. Mawer, and F. M. Stenton, *The Place-Names of Northamptonshire*, English Place-Name Society, x, 1933.

[2] Taking Periods I and II together as 'early': in Period I Northamptonshire had a smaller proportion than Leicestershire.

[3] Other orders were involved as depopulators, but not until the fifteenth century, when they followed the same road as lay landlords: the poll-tax figure of 89 for Sulby in 1377 shows that the Premonstratensian abbey tolerated a village alongside it.

[4] P.R.O., E179/155/31.

reckoned the head of a household. The village must have had considerably more households than this, since there was a limit of personal property below which no tax was levied. In Althorp the number of taxpayers recorded was 20 and in Armston 28. No complete coverage of the county has survived from any other lay tax collection prior to 1334; then the whole basis of tax collection was changed and the assessments and names of individuals ceased to be returned to the Exchequer, which became satisfied with the allocation of a single sum representing the quota of a village.[1] Thus Astwell, which had had 35 taxpayers' names returned to the Exchequer in 1301, was assessed at 60s. 9d. in 1334.

Like Oxfordshire, the study of settlement history in Northamptonshire is partially obscured by the fact that the units of taxation were sometimes made up of more than one vill. There are, in fact, degrees of obscurity. The densest blackness reigns when the tax collectors accounted for a place *cum membris* (as they did for 28 places in 1334), without particularizing the names of the member vills. This makes it impossible to use the evidence of 1334 to assert that particular vills were certainly in existence at that moment. The tax collectors for Nassaburgh Hundred, the area centred on Peterborough, were addicted to large units, six separate entries, each *cum membris*, making up the £113 11s. 6d. collected from the Hundred. Similar large units appear in Polebrook Hundred which adjoined Nassaburgh on the south, in the lower Nene valley, and to a lesser degree in Cleyley and Higham Ferrers Hundreds on the south-eastern edge of the county. It was not the poverty of these areas which made the collectors create such large units for collection, since the sum for Nassaburgh was larger than for any other Hundred by more than £40: rather it seems to have been the scattered (and perhaps late) settlement in these areas which impeded the recognition of each settlement as an adult vill. The price to be paid today is the obscurity of settlement history unless the composition of the large tax-units can be indicated from other sources. This can occasionally be done since different tax collections followed different procedures: the list of vills and their lords, the *Nomina Villarum*, drawn up as the basis for the levy of 1316, is usually very explicit, and thirteen of the Hundreds of the county have no *cum membris* entries. However, in Nassaburgh, Polebrook, and Huxloe Hundreds the composite entry predominates again, but not uniformly, so that the 'members' of Deene, unnamed in 1334, are revealed in 1316 as including the now-deserted Kirby.

Apart from the places entered *cum membris*, the *Nomina Villarum* names 297

---

[1] P.R.O., E179/155/3, tabulated in R. E. Glasscock, 'The Distribution of Lay Wealth in South-East England in the Early Fourteenth Century', London Ph.D. thesis (unpublished), 1963, pp. 594–610.

vills in Northamptonshire, and in 1334 the tax assessments record 308 vills by name. It is not unreasonable to assume that vills *cum membris* were made up of clusters of at least three, and on that supposition the 30 *cum membris* entries of 1316 and the 28 of 1334 can be translated into some 90 vills, making a county total of about 400 for the beginning of the fourteenth century to compare with the 300 or so separate vills recorded in 1086.

TABLE I

Vills assessed in 1316 and 1334 but now deserted

	Total no. of vills*	Now deserted	Proportion deserted
Northamptonshire	392	72	18%
Leicestershire	348	52	15%
Oxfordshire	359	91	25%

* Assuming three vills for each *cum membris* entry; this is a conservative figure.

This figure of 400 is the high-water mark of medieval rural settlement in the county. There is nothing in the tax assessments after 1334 to suggest an extension of settlement, and nothing in the general economic history of the Midlands to indicate more than occasional foundations of new villages between the early fourteenth and the early nineteenth centuries. Certainly the net figure is a subtraction and not an addition. How large a subtraction? and at what period after 1334? The magnitude of the loss is set out in Table I, with the figures for neighbouring counties added for comparative purposes.

Three further important questions must now be asked: how much longer after 1334 did these vills survive? were these unfortunate vills smaller or less wealthy than their surviving neighbours? is there any significant distribution of these deserted vills within the county comparable to that observed already for Oxfordshire: that is, does the overall figure of more than one vill in every six conceal important differences in intensity between one part of Northamptonshire and another? To answer each of these questions involves further discussion of the documentary sources available and employed in the compilation of the Gazetteer.

IV

For the purposes of broad exposition the dates of desertion of sites have been divided into five main periods, categorized in the Gazetteer and in other publications of the Research Group as I, II, III, IV, and V, together with the symbol N when the date is still uncertain; if the date, although uncertain, lies probably within a period, it may be categorized as N followed by a period in brackets: for example Foxley has a Gazetteer entry of N (IV).

Two of these periods, I (mentioned only in Domesday Book) and II (*c.* 1100–*c.* 1350) have already been discussed, and it has been shown that a very small proportion of Northamptonshire sites were deserted in these early periods. It is not until Period III (*c.* 1350–*c.* 1450) that substantial numbers appear, and it is in Period IV (*c.* 1450–*c.* 1700) that desertions proliferate. It is in these periods that the documentary evidence becomes more abundant, although, as the 24 N entries show, it has not yet been able to answer all the questions of dating.

Period III begins with the years of the Black Death, continues through the decades when the plague returned, but stops, *c.* 1450, just short of the years when the great impact of the demand for wool made itself felt in the traditionally corn-growing counties. Its depopulations are therefore likely to be those most closely connected with a fall in English population, and the retreat from marginal land as holdings became available by the death of villagers on more easily worked and more rewarding soils. Since the Black Death is an event well known even to those with little knowledge of the Middle Ages it is natural for it to be frequently blamed in popular tradition for the massive depopulation of Midland villages. Table III shows that the proportion of all desertions that can be definitely or probably assigned to the whole of Period III is 17 per cent, more than in Leicestershire but less than in Oxfordshire.

The documentary basis for assigning a depopulation to Period III is sometimes an explicit statement, such as that made to the Pope in 1412 that the pestilences had robbed Elkington of all its parishioners except three or four servants of Pipewell abbey;[1] and the return of 1428 which reported that in Steane parish there were only four households remaining:[2] in 1086 there had been sixteen, and in 1301 also at least sixteen; in 1334 the vill had paid 40s. 4d. in tax, and even in 1377 there were 51 persons over the age of sixteen years who paid the poll tax. Sulby had been even larger: in 1377 there were 89 taxpayers, but to this parish a mere four households were ascribed in 1428. Stuchbury had 59 taxpayers in 1377 but thereafter very little is heard of the vill. Even more mysterious is the fate of *Torpel* in Bainton. It cannot have been a ghost vill since a charter for a market and fair was granted in 1264,[3] and ten virgates were recorded in 1276; eight taxpayers appear in the roll of 1301 and there were 21 tenants working the demesne in 1329: yet the *Nomina Villarum* and the assessments of 1334 ignore the vill, and the poll-tax collectors also passed it by; "not on the map" is its obituary in the *Place-Names of Northamp-*

[1] *Calendar of Papal Letters*, VI, 1904, p. 393.

[2] The references to material from the years 1086, 1301, 1316, 1334, 1377, 1428, 1524, 1674, and 1841 are given in the introduction to the Gazetteer, pp. 32–3 below.

[3] *Calendar of Charter Rolls*, II, 1906, p. 49.

tonshire.[1] Wythemail is another vill that appears in the *Nomina Villarum* but virtually nowhere else: yet excavation of one of its crofts and the revelation of others by the bulldozer (p. 28 below) again show that this was no ghost village.

Period IV is the classic period when villages were deserted not by the migration of disgruntled tenants seeking better terms elsewhere, but by the landlords evicting their tenants in order to turn arable land over to grazing. In 1377 there were 90 taxpayers in Fawsley, and in the early fifteenth century the Knightleys were having trouble with their demesne tenants who found the services imposed on them too irksome.[2] By the end of the fifteenth century the boot was on the other foot: the reluctant tenants were being evicted by the Knightleys. The church and the great house stand alone in the parkland, and the marks of former ploughlands dip down to the edge of the lakes that flood the little valleys: it is not certain whether the site of the village lies under the waters or under the Hall and gardens.[3] In the mid-sixteenth century 2,500 sheep grazed the site, and the profits of grazing contributed to the large sums to which the two Knightleys living at Fawsley were assessed in the lay taxation of 1524.

The musters of archers, billmen, and horse-harness carried out in 1539 and 1542 were not concerned with the total population of each village, but there is a clear difference between the ordinary village and the deserted townships.[4] Thus, Steane had only three men when other local villages mustered from eleven to 25; Elkington had one, Barford had one, and Elmington had one.

The evidence for the depopulations of this period goes further than the contrast between substantial numbers of taxpayers in 1377 and small numbers assessed in the early sixteenth century, for Northamptonshire was one of the counties most affected by the search for evidence to be used against the grazing landlords which was conducted in 1517–18 and again in 1548–9. Northamptonshire and Oxfordshire account for 31 per cent of the prosecutions brought before the Exchequer between 1518 and 1568, and in the anti-enclosure troubles of 1548 and 1607 (spurred on more by grievances such as the inflation and rack-renting) the rioters remembered what had happened in the lifetimes of their fathers and grandfathers, and raised the cry that unless the landlords' appetites were restrained, whole villages would again come tumbling down.[5]

The prosecutions did not always succeed, as Dr Kerridge has shown,[6] and

[1] Gover *et al.*, *op. cit.*, p. 244.   [2] P.R.O., C66/417 m.18d.

[3] There are slight earthworks near the church that may be remains of the former village: the Knightleys' house is now derelict and used as a saw-mill and timber-store.

[4] *Letters and Papers of Henry VIII*, xiv, pt. 1, 1894, pp. 280–1, and xvii, 1900, pp. 504–5.

[5] M. W. Beresford, *The Lost Villages of England*, 1954, pp. 396–403.

[6] E. Kerridge, 'The Returns of the Inquisitions of Depopulation', *Eng. Hist. Rev.*, 1955, pp. 212–28.

the inquisitions published by Leadam reported depopulations that were rarely equivalent to the population of a whole village.[1] What the inquisitions caught were the offences committed after 1488, the earliest date permitted by the Acts of 1489 and 1515 for retrospective punishment of those who converted arable acres and threw down houses of husbandmen. It has been argued elsewhere[2] that the statement made by John Hales was only too true: that the greater part of the decay of townships had taken place before the beginning of the reign of King Henry VII. In 1491 John Rous drew upon Northamptonshire to cite the case of Upper Charwelton and to warn that Lower Charwelton, where there is now only a church and farm, was in mortal danger.[3]

By the sixteenth century the surviving estate records of old Northamptonshire families become more prolific, and the great work of collection and preservation by the Northamptonshire Record Society has ensured that these are available to scholars. Where villages had once stood, sixteenth-century rentals account for the grazing rents from *Old Town Pasture*, or from a *Townefyld* such as that in a rental of 1539.

There is a considerable gap in time between the poll-tax returns of 1377, when so many Northamptonshire villages that are now deserted can be shown to be occupied, and the allegations of 1517–18 with their glance backwards to 1488. In many ways these are the dark decades, if not the dark age, of medieval documentation: few private estate records survive from the fifteenth century; the Crown and the great monastic landowners had followed the fashion and ceased to be closely involved in the day-to-day farming operations on their estates, taking on instead the rôle of rentiers. With this change, the rentals and other estate documents become less and less informative.

The general decline in population produced two acknowledgements that old bases of taxation needed to be revised. First, in 1428 a return was made of all parishes with fewer than ten households: in other counties the absence of a village from this list is a fair presumption that it was not as yet deserted, but unfortunately the return from Northamptonshire deals with only two deaneries. Nor was a small population in 1428 a guarantee that a village was near its death: Hardwick and Strixton appear in the return but are still villages, and the four houses in Glendon and Barford parish in 1428 do not indicate imminent depopulation, for there were twelve houses in Glendon in 1514 when the graziers fell upon it, and when Barford was destroyed in 1515 it had six houses standing.

---

[1] I. S. Leadam, *The Domesday of Inclosures*, 1897, I, pp. 261–318, and M. W. Beresford, *op. cit.*, p. 402; returns from 1526 are to be found in P.R.O., C47/7/2/3 mm. 1–7.

[2] M. W. Beresford, *op. cit.*, pp. 148–50.

[3] John Rous, *Historia Regum Angliae*, ed. T. Hearne, 1745.

Secondly, from 1433 the Exchequer allowed deductions to be made from a village's tax assessment, as fixed in 1334, if the village was impoverished or depopulated by plague and economic contraction. Several such reduced assessments survive, but there are no strikingly high reliefs allowed in Northamptonshire which would enable deserted sites to be assigned to the period between the poll taxes of 1377 and these *deductiones*.[1] From the mid-fifteenth century the *deductiones* became conventionalized, and the next opportunity afforded by lay taxation records to assess the fate of a village is the re-assessment of 1524. Thus the 23 families at Newbottle in 1301 had been reduced to three taxpayers in 1524, giving substance to the accusations made in 1517 that six houses in the former village had been destroyed by Lord Grey in 1488, probably the final stage of a depopulation that went back beyond 1488. In contrast, Nunton may be cited, for the eleven taxpayers of 1524 make it very unlikely that the village had yet disappeared, although by *c.* 1720 there were only four families in the whole township, and not all of these were living on the former village site. Similarly, the nine taxpayers at Upton in 1524, although considerably fewer than those of 1301 (when there were 49), show that the death of the village was yet to come.

The final occasion when the records of taxation can be utilized for the purpose of tracking down the date of a depopulation comes in the reign of Charles II, when the counting of hearths for the purpose of the Hearth Tax gives an indication of the number and size of houses in each place. These returns do not exist for every place in the Gazetteer, but where available will be found after the date 1674. Thus Walcot, which had 40 taxpayers over the age of sixteen in 1377, was reduced to two houses in 1674, but Upton had still thirteen. The 59 taxpayers of Stuchbury in 1377 were succeeded by the four houses of 1674, and the eleven (? families) recorded in Domesday Book in 1086 at Burghley by Stamford were succeeded by the single house of 70 hearths in 1674.

The pursuit of village names through successive tax assessments is not the only way of tracing the fate of village populations; many other classes of document are capable of indicating the presence or absence of populations. The records of the central government are far from being exhausted,[2] and in recent years two other important classes of document have become more easily available for study. The work of county Record Societies and Record Offices (of which Northamptonshire can be reckoned a pioneer) has made available the private estate records of the landed families, great and small, that made Tudor Northamptonshire a "heralds' garden", while the archives of the diocese have

---

[1] P.R.O., E179/155/105 and 109.

[2] E.g. P.R.O., SC12/13/29: rental of Barford and Glendon, 1327; SC12/13/25: terrier of Evenley and Astwick, temp. Henry VIII.

been shown to include such classes as Tithe Causes and Glebe Terriers that are capable of indicating whether land was anciently enclosed to the accompaniment of evictions.

It is quite clear that depopulating enclosure did not continue in Northamptonshire after 1518 although the phrase was much employed even at the end of the seventeenth century. Enclosure there was in plenty, as Miss Finch's studies of five particular families show, but in this period its aim had ceased to be the acquisition of pastures so extensive that there was no room for a village and villagers. The troubles of 1548–9 and 1607 left no doubt that public opinion and the government were hostile to total depopulation. As Francis Tresham observed in 1604, "you could not remove all the tennantes without much clamor, and especiallie when itt is neare Northampton whose affectiones arr well knowen to you."[1] Depopulation there certainly was, in a restricted sense, for improvement often involved economies in the use of labour and a reduction in the number of tenants, but authentic cases of total depopulation are very few, despite the confusing use of *depopulation* in the title of commissions raised against enclosers by James I and Charles I. As Miss Finch has shown, the fact that an enclosure was made by agreement between the proprietors did not save enclosers from the risk of an appearance in Star Chamber, Exchequer, or before the Privy Council. Laud's Commissioners for Depopulation fined Lord Brudenell £1,000 for an agreed enclosure at Hougham where "his claim rings true that he had 'not a mannor house without a familie, nor a messuage less then hee was left, nor a farmer without his auntient quantitie or sufficient support, nor a cottager without livelyhood, nor an impotent man without releife.' His inclosures had been effected by mutual agreement in the way contemporaries advocated as ideal."[2]

Period V, the years after *c.* 1700, includes the publication of Oliver Goldsmith's poem, *The Deserted Village*, with its shadowy location and vague denunciations. The period's depopulations are almost exclusively those connected with the making of parkland round great country houses. Coming so late, the events are usually well documented, although the thoroughness of landscape gardening or the extensiveness of stables and outbuildings may completely obscure any physical remains of a village. The church often survives in these circumstances, sometimes being annexed to the country house as virtually a private chapel and mausoleum for the landowner's family and servants. The dispossessed villagers were sometimes rehoused in a new village on a site out of view of the house, as at Brockhall and Edgcote. At the latter site

[1] M. E. Finch, *Five Northamptonshire Families, 1540–1640*, Northants. Rec. Soc., XIX, 1956, p. 89, citing British Museum, Add. MS. 39829, ff. 61–3.
[2] M. E. Finch, *op. cit.*, pp. 162–3.

the rectory stands loyally by the church in the park. At Hothorpe John Cook demolished the four remaining cottages of the village *c.* 1830 but rehoused the cottagers in Theddingworth. The houses of Lilford were demolished in 1755 and rebuilt in Wigsthorpe: the parish church was demolished as superfluous *c.* 1780 and its arches put to more practical use as picturesque ruins in a riverside scene. Overstone was transferred to its present site *c.* 1820 and it is interesting to see that permanence could not be assured to a Northamptonshire village even so late as the third decade of the nineteenth century. Table II gathers together from the Gazetteer the periods of desertion conjectured for each site, and Table III adds the comparable percentages from the published data for Oxfordshire and Leicestershire. The documentation available for these three counties varies in quality, with consequent effects on the 'Uncertain' categories. If the most probable view is taken, as in Table III, there still remains about the same proportion of uncertainties in Northamptonshire as in Leicestershire,

TABLE II

Periods of desertion of Northamptonshire villages

Period I (soon after 1086)	4 (5%)
Period II (*c.* 1100–*c.* 1350)	1 (1%)
Period III (*c.* 1350–*c.* 1450)	10 (12%)
Period IV (*c.* 1450–*c.* 1700)	34 (41%)
Period V (after *c.* 1700)	9 (11%)
Uncertain but probably II	—
Uncertain but probably III	4 (5%)
Uncertain but probably IV	15 (19%)
Totally uncertain date	5 (6%)
Total	82 villages

TABLE III

Probable periods of desertion in three Midland counties

	Northamptonshire %	*Leicestershire* %	*Oxfordshire* %
Period I (soon after 1086)	5	8	1
Period II (*c.* 1100–*c.* 1350)	1	8	8
Period III (*c.* 1350–*c.* 1450)	17	12	30
Period IV (*c.* 1450–*c.* 1700)	60	60	45
Period V (after *c.* 1700)	11	5	3
Totally uncertain	6	7	13
Total	82 villages	65 villages	101 villages

but almost twice this proportion in Oxfordshire where the enclosing land-lords appeared less often in Exchequer, King's Bench, and Star Chamber; and where there has been no county historian to study the topography of parishes as John Bridges served Northamptonshire and John Nichols Leicestershire.

Nevertheless the high proportion of depopulations—60 per cent—that can be ascribed to the period 1450–1700 is exactly the same in Northamptonshire as in Leicestershire; Northamptonshire has more depopulations in Periods III and V but fewer in the early periods. Oxfordshire appears as a county with its depopulations more evenly spread between Periods III and IV.

v

In the Oxfordshire study it was shown that the deserted villages, before their depopulation, were generally smaller or less wealthy than their neighbours, although examples were not lacking of vills that were average or above average in these respects. The data for Northamptonshire in 1334 and 1377 are set out in Tables V–VI but it must be realized that information in these terms is not available for all the deserted vills. Quite apart from the composite *cum membris* entries already described (p. 8), the tax collectors often grouped together vills in a single assessment. These linked entries differ from the *cum membris* entries in that the partners are specifically stated, but the assessments or popula-tions of each partner cannot be determined from the documents: for example, Appletree was taxed with Aston le Walls in 1301 and 1334, with 23 taxpayers in the first instance and an assessment of 54s. 9d. in the second; similarly, in the poll tax collection of 1377, 66 persons over fourteen years of age were said to reside in this pair of vills.

Thus Table V can deal only with the 13 deserted vills that were treated separately by the tax collectors of 1334. In three cases both partners in a joint assessment happen to have been deserted: in such cases the sums can properly be included in the calculation of averages, and for the purpose of examining the size-ranges in Tables V and VI such joint assessments have been arbi-trarily divided by two. From 1377, data for 19 separate vills and one pair are available. Taking 1334 and 1377 together, information is available for 28 vills, or 37 per cent of the deserted vills. Since, in general, it was small vills that the tax collectors linked together in joint assessments, the figures in Tables V and VI must refer to the better-off and more populous of the vills that were to be depopulated.

This caution must be reiterated whenever one cites the data in the two Tables, for the Tables themselves already show that the vills which were later to be deserted were already regarded as less wealthy than average in 1334 and less populous than average in 1377. The average Northamptonshire village paid 93s. tax in 1334, and none of the to-be-deserted villages was assessed to as great a sum; the average to-be-deserted village paid 40 per cent of the county average. In 1377, when the average Northamptonshire village had 140 tax-payers over the age of fourteen years, no to-be-deserted village had so many; of the villages in our Gazetteer with surviving poll-tax data, the average number of taxpayers in 1377 was 43 per cent of the number in the average village of the county.

It must now be emphasized (as for Oxfordshire and Leicestershire) that the taxation data not only demonstrate the relative smallness of the villages that were later to be depopulated but also enable us to make two other firm and important observations. First: although small, these vills were not pygmies by the standards of fourteenth-century England, for a payment of 36s. 5d. in 1334 was above the average of all the vills in Nottinghamshire, not to speak of the North and West Ridings of Yorkshire; similarly, in 1377 an average of 60 taxpayers is about the same as that for all vills in these two Ridings of York-shire, and nearly twice the average for Northumberland.

Secondly: this relative smallness of the to-be-deserted vills was not a product of the Black Death. It was as much present in 1334, fifteen years before the plagues, as in 1377. How much further back than 1334 is a more difficult question to answer in the absence of the Hundred Rolls of 1279 for Northamp-tonshire. The information from the tax of 1301 survives for 34 places in the Gazetteer, which is considerably more than have data for 1334. The average number of taxpayers in the deserted vills was 18 in 1301, and the median was 16: considering that the tax of 1301 was assessed on movable property, and that the poorest were exempt, villages with these numbers were not minute, and the 49 taxpayers in Upton and the 44 in Fawsley must indicate quite sub-stantial settlements. Until more work has been done on the non-deserted villages' performance in 1301 it is not possible to say more: the publication of the 1301 assessment would be a very useful work for the county Record Society to undertake.

Domesday Book gives populations for 38 of the deserted vills: again, in the absence of a study of the population of all Northamptonshire villages in 1086, it is impossible to make comparisons between the size of the to-be-lost and the survivors at this early date. In absolute terms, the average recorded popula-tion in the to-be-deserted vills was 12, and it is reasonable to assume that the numbers recorded in Domesday Book were those of the heads of households, and that the average vill contained four or five times this number of people, at least. The comparable figures for Oxfordshire and Leicestershire appear in Table IV; and the Northamptonshire desertions seem to have been generally smaller in 1086 than those of the neighbouring counties, but here again it must

TABLE IV

Size in 1086 of vills later to be deserted

Recorded population	*Percentage of vills in each size-range*		
	Northamptonshire %	*Oxfordshire* %	*Leicestershire* %
1–10	48	42	39
11–20	43	38	36
21–30	8	11	19
31–40	0	7	3
41–50	0	2	0
51–60	0	0	3
Number of deserted vills with data	38	45	36
Total number of deserted vills	82	101	65

TABLE V

Size-range of tax assessments of Northamptonshire villages, 1334

Size of tax quota in shillings	*Percentage of all vills (392 in number)*	*Percentage of to-be-deserted vills (19 in number)*
0– 10	0	5
11– 20	1	15
21– 30	0	10
31– 40	7	30
41– 50	11	10
51– 60	13	10
61– 70	14	5
71– 80	11	10
81– 90	6	0
91–100	12	0
101–110	5	0
111–120	6	0
121–130	3	0
131–140	3	0
141–150	1	0
over 150	7	0
	average quota in each vill: 93s.	average quota in each deserted vill: 36s. 5d.

TABLE VI

Size-range of Northamptonshire vills in 1377

Number of taxpayers over age 14	Percentage of all vills (263 in number)	Percentage of to-be-deserted vills (21 in number)
0– 10	0	0
11– 20	1	15
21– 30	1	20
31– 40	3	10
41– 50	3	5
51– 60	7	30
61– 70	7	0
71– 80	4	0
81– 90	7	15
91–100	7	10
101–110	10	0
111–120	2	0
121–130	6	0
131–140	6	0
141–150	3	0
over 150	33	0
	average number in each vill: 140	average in each deserted vill: 60

be emphasized that the data are available for a little less than half the vills concerned.

It will also be seen from the Gazetteer that it was not the smallest vills in 1086 that fell first: the smallest populations in 1086 were at Hothorpe, Hale, and Snorscomb, yet none of these had disappeared by 1350. Two deserted villages had recorded populations in 1086 of 14 and 18 (probably as many families); and among the seven early desertions in Leicestershire there were vills with 24, 17, and 14 recorded population in 1086. Being small in 1086 was clearly not a fatal obstacle to growth nor a prescription for rapid desertion: but being small in 1301 and 1334 was more perilous.

It would have been interesting to follow the example of Table VIII in the Oxfordshire study (where the least wealthy villages of 1334 were traced back to 1279 and 1086), even though for Northamptonshire the comparisons would have to be with 1301, but it is not only the absence of data from 1279 which stands in the way: of the two deserted vills with assessments under 20s. in 1334, only one (Boughton) appeared in Domesday Book (11 people recorded); and of the seven deserted vills with ten or fewer taxpayers in 1301, only one

(Burghley) appears in Domesday Book (again, with 11 recorded). None of these eight was recorded in 1377, and the group may therefore be characterized as late arrivals, not growing very large, and becoming small after the Black Death. Three of the seven have been assigned Period III dates for desertion, but the others are either IV or N(IV) since there is documentary evidence of prosecution for depopulation in the 1450–1550 period.

VI

The reconnaissance in documents and the field has produced 82 sites. The first list published in 1954 suggested 73 villages, some of which were proposed only on *prima facie* evidence, or as examples of shrunken sites. Subsequent field-work and examination of further documents has eliminated seventeen of these suggestions: on the other hand, the scrutiny of further documents (mainly carried out for the Group by Mrs Betty Grant) has brought to light 26 more sites.

The contribution that Northamptonshire can now be seen to make to the total for the Midland counties is indicated in Table VII, although the figures for Bedfordshire and Huntingdonshire are in advance of a revision of the Group's provisional county lists. Northamptonshire by area occupies 12 per cent of the 'Midlands' as so defined, and its 82 sites make up the same proportion of the 650 sites that are known. In this sense it is absolutely typical. The intensity of desertion was not the same in all Midland counties, but Northamptonshire almost exactly matches Leicestershire and Rutlandshire in having 1·3 desertions for every 10,000 acres. Calculations such as these, dealing with counties as a whole, must immediately make the local student wish for something that indicates differences between the regions of a county. The distribution map printed as a fore-paper is a first step, and a few comments on the pattern may be made, even though a few sites remain unexactly located. The end-paper shows the distribution of sites of different periods, although the number of *Uncertain Period* symbols is a sufficient warning that it is still premature to pursue the correlation of time and place very far.

The first folding map has areas void of deserted villages that are as marked and as extensive as the empty area of the Chilterns in the corresponding Oxfordshire map.

The empty area in the extreme north-east tip of the county consists of fen-land, thinly scattered with medieval villages, and each village large and economically unthreatened by movements in the price of animal products relative to that of cereals; the next area of immunity from desertion is that of Rockingham Forest where only Kirby and Cotes break the gap from Wothorpe to Boughton; and with Rockingham may be joined the much smaller area of

Whittlewood Forest in the south-west of the county, south of the Tove. These forested areas, lightly settled and lowly assessed in 1086, were the home of neither nucleated villages nor extensive tracts of open fields. Their scattered settlements had economies that did not rely completely on the plough, and their small fields were not tempting to those graziers whose flocks ran to thousands.

TABLE VII

Number and intensity of deserted villages in
Northamptonshire and eight neighbouring counties

	Number of desertions	Area of county (0,000 acres)	Intensity per 10,000 acres
Northampton	82	63	1·3
Bedford	15	30	0·5
Buckingham	45	47	0·9
Huntingdon	18	23	0·8
Leicester	67	51	1·3
Lincoln	181	176	1·0
Oxford	101	47	2·1
Rutland	13	9	1·4
Warwick	127	57	2·2
Total	649	503	1·3

The great blank area on the map in the Nene valley, centring on Northampton, is difficult to explain. No similar shadow of immunity was thrown by the county towns of Oxford, Leicester, or Buckingham; one would require to know more about the distribution of old-enclosed arable in the county before venturing to comment on this interesting and puzzling immunity, which seems to extend to that part of the Northampton Heights that lay north of the county town.[1] Otherwise the Northampton Heights have depopulated sites as close-packed as anywhere in England, close neighbours to those of the *Felden*, the valley of the Warwickshire Avon, where depopulation aroused the spirited anger of John Rous in the late fifteenth century, and near where Oxfordshire marches with Warwickshire and Northamptonshire at the Three Shire Stones. These were graziers' grounds *par excellence*, the home territory of the Knightleys and the Spencers.

The mention of individuals rather than physical regions returns us to a proper emphasis on the local factors determining whether or not a particular village was depopulated. Perhaps everyone who draws a distribution map of

[1] The influence of the leather industry may have favoured cattle rather than sheep: cattle need more man-power than sheep.

deserted villages should be compelled to add in some brilliant colour the villages that have *not* been deserted. Such an addition would reiterate that even in areas where desertion was frequent, and where physical factors of soil and settlement seem to have tempted or forced depopulation, there were villages with similar soil and similar settlement where the landlord was not tempted or where the husbandmen were able to resist eviction. These differences bring us back to the true variety of English local history and to the true multiplicity of factors that operate human decisions at all periods. The sites identified, a close study of the personnel of landlords and tenants at the crucial periods is as obvious a task for local students as the close study of the siting of each deserted village in relation to water and soil, and of the agrarian economies that were operated in the fields and that sustained the life of the community when it was still a medieval village.

VII

Documentary proof that a village once existed is one thing: the discovery of the site quite another. Since the greater part of the desertions occurred before the making of large-scale county maps there is no medieval cartographic equivalent of the *Nomina Villarum* and the tax assessment rolls. Occasionally, large-scale Tudor plans such as those commissioned at an exchange of lands at Kirby in 1584 and 1587 show the vestiges of the village and its final submergence under the gardens of the Hall.[1] In 'the survey of the mannor of Kyrby' dated 1584, a few houses remained on the west of the Hall, but the long main street that once ran up the side of the hill south of the Hall was completely empty: it is here that the earthworks of the street, houses, and crofts can now be clearly seen in the grass. The field on the east of the empty street was labelled *Kirby Croftes*, and the still unenclosed block of open-field arable to the west was named *the furlong by the townes side*. A plan of 1587, 'the survaye of the mannor of Kyrby', shows that the Brudenell holding in the furlong had been assigned to the owner of Kirby and that the furlong was now enclosed, and likewise *Kyrby Crofte*: a third plan, 'Woodes in Greatton', also of 1587, shows that the Hall grounds were being enlarged at this time so as to extend over the few houses of the village that had remained on the 1584 plan.

Other estate records may yield one or two plans of this type and period, but the chances are not great. A plan of Overstone, drawn in 1671, shows the village in its old position, before its removal to a new site.[2] By the time that accurate medium-scale county maps, such as that of Jefferys in 1779, came to

---

[1] Northants. Archives Committee: Finch-Hatton MS. 272, ff. 5–7; plans by Ralph Treswell.

[2] Northants. Archives Committee: 'Map of the Manor of Overstone belonging to Benjamin Mildmay, Lord Fitzwalter, 1671': this reference is by kindness of Mr P. I. King.

be drawn, the majority of deserted villages had already perished. Jefferys, like
the more recent Ordnance Survey maps, showed Faxton as a fully occupied
site, but the late desertion here must be regarded as a freak with only one or
two parallels in the whole country.

By the time of the first edition of the 6-inch Ordnance Survey maps in
1880–7 the memory of village sites in Northamptonshire had faded, and none
of the earthworks caught the attention of the surveyors. One wonders how they
ignored the deep indentation of Kirby village street and the high-banked earthworks of the houses and crofts. The private map-makers of the eighteenth
century were also indifferent to deserted village sites in the county, and there
was no parallel to Henry Beighton's zealous recording of Warwickshire sites,
although the county's historian, John Bridges, was well aware of deserted
village earthworks and of the historical significance of parishes and townships
that lacked any nucleated village settlement. At Barford he noted the former
chapel destroyed and levelled, and "the marks of houses still apparent from
the face of the ground," while at Furtho "the remains of a former village are
still to be seen;" at Glassthorpe, "tradition and the broken appearance of the
ground point out Great Bury Field as the spot where the village formerly
stood," and at Kingsthorpe he saw "hollow places with marks and foundations
of a village." His account of Nobold deserves quotation in full. "Throughout
the whole of Old Nobold Close are many irregular banks and hollows, such as
are usual in ruinous places, about which have been turned up walling stones
and old hearth-stones, as supposed from the marks they bore of fire. Round
these heaps and hollows are partition banks and ditches, inclosing such extents
of ground as are commonly allotted to the homesteads of cottages and farm-
houses. Nearly the length of the close along the middle of it is a list or tract of
ground, lower than the ground on both sides, which appears to have been
raised by rubbish, supposed to have been the principal street of the town.
Upon boring into it in several places the stick was checked as by a stone causey
about three inches below the surface. In one part is a plot of ground immediately called the church-yard, and a large old tree growing in it, lately cut
down, always called the churchyard tree. Human skulls and bones have been
dug up here. There are also fords and tracts of roads still remaining which led
here from other towns."[1] These are exactly the symptoms which can still be
expected in the unploughed fields of a Northamptonshire site of first quality.

At Walton, two hundred years before Bridges, Leland had noticed the
chapel "defaced and taken down;" the name had been preserved in *Chapel
Field* which Bridges located as "on the right hand as you go into King's Sutton
Field." The ruins of a church or the tradition of a graveyard are a good guide

[1] John Bridges, *History and Antiquities of Northamptonshire*, ed. of 1791, ii, p. 23.

to the site of a village, since the normal place for a church was near the houses. An isolated church is not always a sign of a desertion or a migration, it must be stressed: had Maxey or Harrington been deserted, for example, it would be quite useless to search for the village in the field adjoining the isolated church.

If there is no church as a guide, the natural place to begin to search for the characteristic earthworks, such as Bridges described at Nobold, would be near the house, Hall, or farm that still bears the name of the village, should such appear on the map. For this purpose the first edition of the 6-inch Ordnance Survey map is the best. Sometimes the name of a former village is preserved in the name of the pastures or *grounds* that replaced it, as at Walton Grounds. While in general the farm with the name of a former village is a good point of departure in a search, it can sometimes happen that any time in the last two centuries a farm has been rebuilt on a fresh site, taking with it the name of its predecessor, and hence the name of the village. Thus the houses and farms called Sulby, Elkington, and Astwick do not lead enquirers to the sites of these villages: Bridges saw the site of Astwick away from the present farm, and recorded its position; Sulby is not at Sulby Hall, Sulby Lodge, Sulby Covert, or Sulby Grange: the site was discovered in an isolated position in the course of one of Dr St Joseph's aerial sorties. The site of Nobold in Clipston, a first-class set of earthworks, was represented by no modern field-name, wood-name, or farm-name; nor was it in the large hundred-acre field of a type which elsewhere has pointed to an early and unfragmented enclosure for grazing: Dr St Joseph found the site in another field to the north.

The availability of the R.A.F. air cover and the more recent selective surveys by Dr St Joseph have greatly facilitated the identification of difficult sites, as well as the interpretation of features at well-known sites. A visit on foot to every field in a civil parish is a long operation, quite apart from difficulties of access and trespass. The air photograph trespasses painlessly for all parties but even the air photograph may fail to reveal a site in unfavourable conditions of light, shadow, soil disturbance, or crop coloration, and repeated visits may be necessary to obtain a clear confirmatory view.

The area of a deserted village and its fields has sometimes produced an irregular shape, usually a protuberance, in the parish to which it has been amalgamated, and thus the area of enquiry is narrowed (e.g. the 'tail' of Apethorpe parish on the south-west, protruding into Southwick and Woodnewton, that contains Halefields Farm and the site of Hale where Bridges noticed "vestiges of three long streets"). Yet there are also protuberances which seem to have been isolated manors and not villages, such as the areas centred on Buscott in Higham Ferrers and upon Walcot in Fotheringhay.

The location of a site can sometimes be determined by the confluence of green lanes or of footpaths, such as those that converge on the river-crossing and former village at Trafford, while the former road-system converging on Walton (in King's Sutton) includes the track anciently known as the Port Way. It was one of John Rous's complaints against enclosing depopulators that the destruction of a village caused roads to be diverted outside the pastures to the inconvenience of travellers, and he specifically instanced Charwelton. The enclosure of Furtho in 1600 caused the Northampton road to be diverted, the village removed, and a church built on a new site: a century later Bridges saw the vestiges of the village along the course of the old road.

The surveyors who drew the maps that accompanied the Tithe Awards had no brief to make a record of archaeological features, but their maps sometimes afford useful pointers to the position of a village site within a township. In some cases it is the record of the field-name that does the service; and in others it is the fact that old-enclosed land was already exonerated from tithe so that a blank area within a parish, ignored by the surveyors, indicates where the fields of a deserted village once lay. 'Old enclosures' on a map from the period of Parliamentary enclosure can sometimes serve the same end. Mr J. W. Anscomb has noticed that the Byfield Enclosure Award of 1779 included a transfer of land to the rector as recompense for the tithes of "Trafford Grounds," and a plan of these Grounds was appended to the Award. Among the twenty fields making up the area of Trafford was no. 10, *Old Town*, a 23-acre field broken only by two spinneys and containing a single farm-building. There had been six families in Trafford in 1086, thirteen taxed in 1301, but no separate record in the tax assessments after 1316 when it was usually taxed jointly with Byfield. The Tithe Award for Astwick has the significant field-name *Stoneheap Ground* at the village site, and it is noteworthy that the only field not under the plough when the Tithe Award was made was this field with its stubborn remains.

Where a site has been identified, the quality of the surviving earthworks (and the date of the inspection) are given in the Gazetteer. It is thus possible for local students to pick out good-quality examples to visit before undertaking their own search for the sites not yet identified. (With the gathering force of the ploughing-up campaign they may need to hurry if they are to beat the bulldozer that has already visited Downtown, Kingsthorpe, and Wythemail. Only a minority of six sites are scheduled as Ancient Monuments, and the amount of *de facto* protection that scheduling offers is not encouraging.) No claim is made that every field in the empty townships has been visited, and where the R.A.F. photographs were taken in unfavourable conditions it has not been possible to go further: nor have Dr St Joseph's commitments allowed him to fly over every field. There may be a Nobold awaiting its first visitor on the ground, although it is more likely that the sites unidentified (U in the Gazetteer) are concealed simply because their earthworks are slight or because crop marks reveal themselves only with particular crops, and then seasonally. It is also possible that some sites classed as D (no visible remains at site) will turn out to be false trails, a better quality site lying elsewhere than near the farm that bears the village name.

TABLE VIII

Visual quality of sites of different periods

Period of desertion	Visual quality of sites						
	A*	A	B	C	D	U	Total
In Domesday Book only	–	–	–	–	–	4	4
c. 1100–c. 1350	–	–	–	–	–	1	1
c. 1350–c. 1450	–	3	2	2	–	3	10
c. 1450–c. 1700	–	5	11	11	3	4	34
After c. 1700	–	1	1	4	3	–	9
Unknown period	–	6	6	11	1	–	24
Total	0	15	20	28	7	12	82

Table VIII shows the relation between the visible quality of a site and its period of desertion. As one might expect, the older desertions remain the most difficult to trace, although the excavation of one of these early desertions would be of prime interest. The single Period II desertion is also untraced. With Period III there are three first-class sites—or rather, there were when the Gazetteer was compiled—and a moderate selection from Periods IV and V. It should be noticed that difficulty in dating a site from documents does not mean that the site is of poor visual quality: six first-class sites are of Unknown Period. Conversely, some sites that are of good quality as earthworks (e.g. Braunstonbury) are poorly documented; Wythemail, with about thirty houses on the ground, appears only in the *Nomina Villarum*; the only reference to Kirby in Blakesley, the site of which was noticed by Bridges on the ground, is also the *Nomina Villarum*. Places such as *Chilcote*, with the tiny Domesday population of two, or Fawcliff, with evidence for neither its population nor its taxable value, have been excluded from the Gazetteer. Table IX compares Northamptonshire with its neighbours: there is little significant difference.

TABLE IX

Visual quality of sites in Northamptonshire and two neighbouring counties

	A*	A	B	C	D	U	Total
	%	%	%	%	%	%	
Northamptonshire	–	18	25	35	8	15	82
Oxfordshire	2	12	28	32	16	11	101
Leicestershire	5	18	18	33	8	17	65

VIII

It might be thought that archaeologists would have flocked to excavate the sites of Unknown Period that had first-class visible remains. This has not been so: and there are some reasons for the apparent neglect. In the first place, if the aim of an excavation was to ascertain when a village was deserted, nothing less than excavation of the total area could determine this date. Excavation of single houses or of a sample of houses might show that all the pottery came from before (say) 1350, but there would still be the possibility that the unexcavated part of the village was occupied after that date. Excavation of the total area of a village would be a very formidable task both in time and energy. The second hard fact, however, is that monies for research excavation are very difficult to come by in England, and the funds at the disposal of the Inspectorate of Ancient Monuments (themselves limited) have to be shared between sites of all periods from the Stone Age onwards that are threatened by destruction; and these are not necessarily the sites whose excavation would add most to knowledge. Even the threatened sites have not been totally excavated in advance of destruction.

If archaeology is unlikely to be readily available as a means of dating depopulations, what are its uses in deserted village study? As the following note shows, its main importance is in determining the character of peasant houses of different social class, different periods, different agricultural regions, and different availability of natural building materials. Major dynamic questions, such as the total number of houses occupied at different periods, have to be placed in the same category of hopeful deferment as the question of dates for final depopulation: nothing short of total excavation will do. Excavations of manor houses have important things to say about differential standards of living within the same village, and excavations of churches can hint at dynamic expansions and contractions in the numbers of worshippers and in the wealth of those who provided and maintained the fabrics, as well as affording evidence, from skeletal remains, of diet, disease, age of death, and related questions. No manor house or church excavations have yet taken place at a deserted village site in Northamptonshire. The house excavations must now be briefly described.

Unlike Oxfordshire, where only limited excavation had taken place, and that without producing any satisfactory house plans,[1] there have been two larger excavations in Northamptonshire as well as three small ones. The major excavations were carried out by the then Ministry of Works as part of its programme of excavating sample croft-sites on villages threatened with destruction. The greatest current threat to these sites is levelling for agriculture, and

[1] Since *The Deserted Villages of Oxfordshire* went to press the Ashmolean Museum has reported an excavation by Mr Cowling of a house-complex at Dornford (1964–5).

the excavated examples at both Wythemail and Muscott were threatened by the bulldozer.

At Wythemail Mrs D. G. Hurst excavated a croft 85 ft by 75 ft for seven weeks in the autumn of 1954. The major building was a long-house 60 ft long and 15 ft wide. The byre and the living quarters of the house were of the same length but of different construction. The living part had a rough stone foundation for a half-timbered structure and there was a central hearth: but on the lower side of the cross-passage two of the walls of the byre were solidly constructed of stone while the third wall seems to have been of timber. There was a cobbled courtyard in front of the house and small outhouses along one edge of the croft. This building was datable to the thirteenth and early fourteenth centuries.

At Muscott Mr P. Savage excavated a croft for six weeks in the autumn of 1958. Three crofts were threatened, but trial trenches showed stone structures in only one of them. In this croft was a farm-complex comprising three buildings. The living house was 50 ft by 25 ft, built of stone with a central hearth in the living part; its lower area was divided into two long narrow rooms by an axial wall. Traces of a baffle-entrance make it unlikely that this building was used for cattle, and there was not the cross-passage usually found separating the domestic and animal quarters of a long-house. The second building was a barn 40 ft by 20 ft with a central row of posts and four rows of stake-holes suggesting a raised wooden floor. The third building had been largely destroyed but it was 22 ft by 16 ft. The whole complex was dated to the thirteenth and early fourteenth centuries.

Smaller excavations took place in 1909 at Mallows Cotton where Mr C. V. Charlton excavated several structures. Unfortunately neither the records nor pottery from this excavation have survived. In 1948 and 1949 Mr K. A. Franey excavated a series of test holes at Onley. A paved road 15 ft across was found, while on the house-platforms scattered stones, pottery, and nails were found, but no structures. More recent work has shown that such trial trenches are not likely to locate flimsy house foundations. This type of house can be detected only by opening up large areas.

In 1964 the farmer at Silsworth, Mr Gilbert, dug a 65-ft-long section across a road which was shown to be composed of built-up layers of gravel containing twelfth-century pottery, with later clinker and stone roads above. By the side of the road were found the foundations of a thirteenth-century building. No pottery later than the early fourteenth century was found. Trial excavations of this kind are not to be encouraged, since they add very little to knowledge, and trenches dug across features can do a great deal of damage and prevent correct interpretation in any future work. Their limited value lies in giving a date-range to a particular part of a site.

The excavations of complete crofts at Wythemail and Muscott have, how-ever, been of considerable interest and it is unfortunate that reports of neither have as yet been published. Both sites are of normal Midland type in which the village earthworks comprise a series of rectangular raised enclosures with a network of sunken roads. In neither case were any stone foundations visible on or near the surface such as one finds in the Cotswolds, Lincolnshire, and Yorkshire, where building stone is abundant. Nevertheless, on both sites the peasant houses had stone foundations: therefore it cannot be assumed that other Midland sites with earthworks of this type were confined to timber houses only. The presence of cobbled yards can also help to define the limits of vanish-ed timber houses, as has been shown from other sites where stone foundations were not found, e.g. at Thuxton, Norfolk, and Caldecote, Buckinghamshire.

The house plans are also important since they show the presence, in the thirteenth century, both of long-houses, where the cattle and the humans lived under the same roof, and of farms where the different buildings formed separate structures. Recent excavations have shown that the long-house, which was once thought to be confined to the 'Highland Zone', was wide-spread throughout Britain during the medieval period. Yet the excavations at Muscott, and at Seacourt, Berkshire (where there were no long-houses at all)[1] show that this was not the only house-type, and that there were medieval farms as well. More work is clearly needed to determine the significance of these differences but it may be suggested that there were three basic types of medieval peasant house: first, small one- or two-room cottages which would be lived in by cottars; secondly, long-houses which may have belonged to villeins; and thirdly, farms which may have belonged to the more prosperous peasants and to the emerging yeomen farmers.[2]

IX

Part of the difficulty in defining a deserted medieval village arises from the ease with which the deserted village category merges into that of the shrunken village. If totally deserted sites remained unrecognized for so long, despite prominent earthworks alongside ruined or disused churches, it is not surprising that the earthworks of shrunken villages have attracted even less archaeolo-gical attention, although they are even more numerous than those of desertions. Once the eye has become accustomed to the characteristic house-platforms of the clay plains or to the buried walls of houses in the upland stone-belts, it will be constantly drawn to similar signs in the grass beyond the limits of existing

[1] M. Biddle, 'The Deserted Medieval Village of Seacourt, Berkshire', *Oxoniensia*, XXVI–VII, 1961–2, pp. 70–201.

[2] J. G. Hurst, 'The Medieval Peasant House', in A. Small (ed.), *The Fourth Viking Conference*, 1965, pp. 190–6.

villages, in empty crofts within the villages, and alongside disused lanes running out to the former open fields. Their relation to ridge-and-furrow and to the sunken hollow-ways of former field-lanes is usually plain: they are completely integrated with these features of open-field topography. They border the hollow-ways as houses would border a street, and the ridge-and-furrow ends at the boundaries of their crofts just as countless open-field plans show the selions of the furlongs coming to an end, marshalled in line where the hedged garths and crofts of the enclosed house-gardens of the village began. If ever a complete survey is achieved these shrunken villages will probably emerge as the commonest English earthwork of any type or period.

Table X

Some shrunken village sites in Northamptonshire

	Grid reference		Grid reference
Bulwick	TL 963941	Oakley, Great	SP 872856
Deene	TL 953927	Orton	SP 806794
Fotheringhay	TL 062929	Pilton	TL 023844
Halse	SP 566404	Plumpton	SP 598484
Hardwick	SP 850698	Rockingham	SP 866916
Harrington	SP 772804	Stanford on Avon	SP 590789
Helmdon	SP 588433	Stoke Doyle	TL 026863
Hemington	SM 090850	Strixton	SP 902616
Kelmarsh	SP 734794	Welford	SP 640805
Lilbourne	SP 561775	Weston Pinkney	SP 590469
Luddington	TL 105836	Wilbarton	SP 811883

Their historical interpretation is less straightforward since they can arise from a number of different circumstances and periods of agrarian change. They may be no more than the record of the drift from the countryside and the contraction of agricultural employment in the last 150 years: but in this case they should be found on old large-scale maps. They may record the migration of village populations, not to towns but to the isolated farms, set in the newly-enclosed fields, that replaced the houses of the original nucleated village. They may record sites abandoned when improving squires built model dwellings elsewhere or when park-makers moved part of a village to make way for ornamental features. They may, on the other hand, record shrinkages of population as old as the decades following the Black Death.

The Oxfordshire essay concluded with some suggestions for further field-work in that county. Those suggestions hold for Northamptonshire, and to them may be added a plea for the investigation of the shrunken sites. The same concluding words may still be employed: it is a long agenda.

GAZETTEER

THE 82 separate entries in the Gazetteer follow a standard pattern. The name of the former settlement is given first, and if there is no modern civil parish of the same name, the parish in which the site now lies is named in brackets: e.g. APPLETREE (in Aston le Walls). Where a civil parish, church, farm, or other feature still bears the settlement name, the spelling employed is that of the 1-inch and 6-inch Ordnance Survey maps: otherwise, the spelling is that of the earliest known reference: e.g. BRIME (in Culworth). The place-name is followed by the sheet number of the 1-inch O.S. map (7th Edition), and then by the two-letter and six-figure National Grid references to the site. If the site has been only approximately located, the map reference is preceded by c. If there is doubt about the suggested location, the map reference is preceded by a question-mark. Where nothing is known beyond the name of the parish in which the site lies, the grid reference will lead to the village of this parish: e.g. CALME (in Clipston, 133 SP 714816). The villages in the Gazetteer are those within the bounds of Northamptonshire in 1964.

Two other important pieces of information are conveyed by standardized abbreviations that follow the six-figure National Grid reference. One series of abbreviations categorizes the period when each site is thought to have been deserted. Five Roman figures are employed for the five main periods and the letter N when the period is still uncertain. This categorization also appears on the end paper map. The broad categories employed are:

I. Early desertion: no reference other than in Domesday Book, 1086.
II. c. 1125 to c. 1350.
III. c. 1350 to c. 1450.
IV. c. 1450 to c. 1700.
V. after c. 1700.
N. uncertain date.

These categories have already been employed in the provisional lists prepared and circulated for most English counties in the *Annual Reports* of the Deserted Medieval Village Research Group, and the division between periods has been made with an eye to separating depopulating forces that operated with different intensity in different periods.

A second series of abbreviations gives the quality of the visible remains of the village and the date when they were last inspected. This classification in terms of field archaeology is based on the following categories and abbreviations:

A* Excellent visual quality: a clear pattern of earthworks recognizable as roads and croft-boundaries, together with the shapes of houses visible under grass, scrub, or woodland.

A   Very good: as A* except for the absence of clear remains of houses: such absence is particularly to be expected where village houses were of timber throughout.

B   Medium quality: good earthworks of roads (hollow-ways), but otherwise imprecise.

C   Poor: either (i) church or church ruins but no earthworks characteristic of houses, crofts, or roads; or (ii) uneven ground and vague bumps only.

D   No visible remains yet traced at the site.

U   Location of site unknown.

The classification is qualified in some entries by an additional abbreviation (in brackets), drawn from the following list.

P   Site now ploughed.

COV   Site thought to lie under a cover of modern farm buildings, ornamental gardens, etc.

VS   Very shrunken: a village that has patently been more extensive but now reduced to six or fewer houses.

M   Removal or migration of village to a new site.

HOU   Site recently re-settled by modern housing: such recent housing is not taken into account in determining a VS site.

The inspection of the sites for this categorization has been the responsibility of Mr J. G. Hurst and was carried out between 1958 and 1964. It should be realized that a change of crop may conceal or reveal a site, and that modern farming practice is increasingly destructive of village earthworks. The site of Mill Cotton, discovered only in 1963 by Mr A. E. Rollings, was levelled almost immediately afterwards. Areas of crofts and house-sites were observed but it was too late to take any other defensive or recording action.

The next part of each Gazetteer entry is made up of a series of dates followed by taxation or population statistics. The choice of these dates is determined by the occasions when the needs of medieval government caused heads to be counted, taxable capacity to be assessed, or villages to be numbered: and, as with all documentary sources, there are the over-riding chance forces that determine whether or not a document has survived the intervening years. Thus, from the valuable collection of the poll tax of 1377 there should be receipts for the groats paid by some 400 Northamptonshire vills: but only 264 will be found in the surviving Exchequer files.

1086. The figure indicates the recorded population in Domesday Book.[1]

1301. The figure indicates the number of taxpayers in the assessment for the lay subsidy.[2]

[1] Data kindly supplied by Prof. H. C. Darby.   [2] P.R.O., E179/155/31.

1316. This date indicates that the vill is mentioned by name in the *Nomina Villarum.*[1]

1334. The sum given is that paid by the whole vill for the lay subsidy, and unless otherwise stated at the rate of one-fifteenth.[2]

1377. The figure indicates the number of taxpayers over the age of 14 years who paid the poll tax.[3]

1428. This entry indicates that the parish was returned as then having fewer than ten households.[4]

1524. The figure indicates the number of taxpayers in the vill in the freshly assessed taxation of the laity.[5]

1674. The figure indicates the number of separate houses in the vill as set out in the returns of the Hearth Tax collectors.[6]

c. 1720. The number of families according to John Bridges, *History and Antiquities of Northamptonshire*, 2 vols., 1791).

1841. Population recorded in the *Census*, the first for which the returns for individual households can be consulted.[7]

Where a vill was joined with one or more neighbours for taxation purposes that fact is stated in the notes following each Gazetteer entry; although these joint entries mask the population or number of taxpayers in the constituent vills, the inclusion of the name of a now-deserted vill is worth noting.

Uncertainties remain after the reconnaissance, concerning the exact date of a desertion, and they derive from the nature and date of the documentary sources themselves. If the taxable wealth of villagers had been re-assessed annually throughout the Middle Ages, or if the poll taxes had been levied more often, or if governments had carried out national censuses, there would be little room for doubt about the date of a depopulation. The most important documents, as we have seen, date from 1086, 1301, 1316, 1334, 1377, 1428, 1524, and 1674: these dates are not regularly spaced, and the enquiries made on each occasion were not uniform.

An example of each type of *Uncertain Period* can be given:

N(I)   This would be a village where there is doubt if a particular Domesday Book entry refers; there is no such case in Northamptonshire.

N(II)   No Northamptonshire villages fall in this category, made up of places with substantial earthworks but only a small number of taxpayers in the early fourteenth-century documents.

N(III) Uncertainty arises when a document for 1377, 1428, 1524, or 1674 fails to mention the place. Thus Badsaddle was not taxed after 1316, nor Perio separately after 1316.

[1] *Feudal Aids and Analogous Documents, 1284–1431*, IV, 1906, pp. 19–30.
[2] P.R.O., E179/155/3.   [3] P.R.O., E179/155/27–9.   [4] *Feudal Aids*, IV, pp. 51–2.
[5] P.R.O., E179/155/122–64.   [6] P.R.O., E179/254/14.   [7] P.R.O., HO107/795–817.

N(IV) A village has low recorded population in 1524 or 1674 but without positive references in intermediate documents to enclosure or depopulation. Thus, Silsworth was reduced to one house by *c.* 1720, but there is no reference in 1524 and 1674 and indeed nothing positive since 1392.

N(V) No village falls into this category as the documentation in the period after *c.* 1700 has fewer gaps.

Thus there still remain villages whose sites elude identification, and depopulations that cannot be firmly dated. There will also be errors and omissions for which the authors must be blamed. This reconnaissance is designed to assist those who alone can make improvement and push forward the frontier of knowledge: those who have access to local documents, and those who can explore the countryside. Corrections, comments, and reports should be sent to the Honorary Secretary of the Deserted Medieval Village Research Group at 67 Gloucester Crescent, London, N.W.1.

ACHURCH (in Thorpe Achurch). 134 TL 022832. N. C(M)(1963).
1301: 28. *c.* 1720: 18.
This village and its hamlet, Thorpe Waterville, together known by 14th cent. as Thorpe Achurch and rarely distinguished. Cottages along both sides of road in 1779 have been rebuilt as single row. Isolated church may indicate earlier site.

ALTHORP. 133 SP 682650. IV. D(COV)(1956).
1086: 10. 1301: 20. 1316. 1377: 51. *c.* 1720: 1. 1841: 55.
Probably taxed with Brington. Owned in 15th cent. by Catesby family. In 1505 manor consisted of 80a. arable, 200a. meadow, 400a. pasture, and 60a. wood; no tenants mentioned. Sold in 1508 to John Spencer of Wormleighton (Warks.). In 1547 flock of 1,200 sheep grazed, and in 1577 Spencers had 4 large pastures here. Now large park with mansion and estate buildings.

APPLETREE (in Aston le Walls). 145 SP 483497. IV. A(VS)(1958).
1316. 1841: 92.
Usually taxed with Aston. Half of Appletree owned with Aston, and half by Chalcombe Priory. In 14th cent. 9 persons with land in open fields. Monastic manor let in 1509, apparently then without tenants. Eight able-bodied men in 1539. 1841 population not at hamlet site. Two farms and one cottage remain.

ARMSTON (in Polebrook). 134 TL 060858. IV. B(VS)(1963).
1301: 28. 1674: 7. *c.* 1720: 4. 1841: 26.
Bought temp. Hen. VIII, with lands of chantry and hospital here, by Sir Edw. Montagu of Boughton (q.v.). Still considerable arable then; 30a. enclosed *c.* 1600, with final enclosure in 1683. *c.* 1720 one house was former chapel. Two farms and 4 cottages remain.

ASHBY, CANONS. 145 SP 578506. IV. B(VS)(1964).
1086: 16. 1301: 18. 1316. 1377: 82. 1524: 21. 1674: 5. *c.* 1720: 6.
1841: 56.
Priory founded in 12th cent. endowed with some land here. Lay manor, with 160a.
arable in demesne in 1353, apparently came later to priory. In 1489 prior enclosed
and converted 100a. to pasture and destroyed 3 houses. Rents paid by 9 tenants in
1535. Manor, already wholly enclosed, came at Dissolution to Sir John Cope, who
kept 2,000 sheep here in 1547. Church, farm, and 4 cottages remain.

ASTWELL (in Helmdon). 145 SP 615430. IV. B(1963).
1086: 17. 1301: 35. 1316. 1334: 60s. 9d. 1377: 57. 1524: 15. 1674: 11.
c. 1720: 4 (Astwell). 1841: 46. (All except 1086 and 1729 are Astwell and Falcutt,
q.v.).
Astwell and Falcutt manors came together in Lovett family in late 15th cent. Thos.
Lovett created deer park in 1547 and kept 300 sheep on Astwell Pasture. 17th-cent.
mansion now mainly demolished. 15th-cent. tower remains with fishponds.

ASTWICK (in Evenley). 145 SP 570342. IV. A(1963).
1316.
Usually taxed with Evenley. Some land belonging to Brackley Hospital (whose
property passed in 1484 to Magdalen College, Oxford) enclosed before 1535. Still
at least 3 houses in 1510. *c.* 1720 overgrown site of manor-house, ruins called "The
Old Town," and 6 scattered farms; large warren had been destroyed *c.* 1670. Site
not at present Astwick Farm.

BADSADDLE (in Orlingbury). 133 SP 833730. N(III). A(1962).
1316.
Rated at 2 ploughs in 1220. Hen. Green bought manor in 1348; in 1392 it consisted
of 20a. meadow, 200a. pasture, and 20a. wood; no arable or tenants mentioned.
Later reverted to common pasture for Orlingbury. In 1547 200 sheep maintained.
Imparked *c.* 1570, causing complaints, and later disparked. *c.* 1720 "a lone house"
with moat filled in. One house remains.

BARFORD (in Rushton). 133 SP 850820. IV. C(1964).
1086: 7. 1316. 1334: 79s. (a Tenth) (with Glendon, q.v.). 1377: 52 (with
Glendon). 1674: 6 (with Glendon). *c.* 1720: 1. 1841: 9.
In 1327 14 tenants. In 1428 whole parish had fewer than 10 households. In 1515 6
houses—"almost the whole village"—destroyed and 86a. enclosed and converted
to pasture by Geo. Boyvile. In 1547 500 sheep maintained. "The marks of houses"
still apparent *c.* 1720. Farm now demolished. Ironstone-working close by.

BOUGHTON (in Weekley). 133 SP 900815. IV. C(1964).
1086: 11. 1316. 1334: 9s. 3½d. 1377: 12. *c.* 1720: 1.
Had two manors. The smaller acquired crenellated mansion and park in 1473, and

was purchased in 1532 by Sir Edw. Montagu. The larger, belonging to Bury St Edmunds Abbey in 1086, was granted away at unknown date and eventually purchased by Montagu. In 1547 600 sheep maintained. *c.* 1720 "foundation stones of buildings" said to have been dug up when bowling green made. Now mansion in park.

BRAUNSTONBURY (in Braunston). 132 SP 531655. IV. A(1955).

Manor belonging to Lilleshall Abbey (Salop.) still tenanted in 1421 when demesnes leased out. At Dissolution these lands sold to earl of Rutland, who already had another manor here. In second manor in 1305 tenants paid rents of £5 0s. 4d. Site completely deserted.

BRIME (in Culworth). 145 SP *c.* 527484. I. U.
1086: 9.

This place has been identified as one of two Culworth manors, in Pinkney Fee. Manor sold *c.* 1300 to owner of second manor. In 1225 guardian of heir to one Culworth manor sued for destruction of manor-house and other houses, but this cannot be clearly identified with Pinkney manor.

BROCKHALL. 133 SP 633626. V. C(VS)(1958).
1086: 6 (with Muscott, q.v.). 1301: 48 (with Muscott). 1316. 1334: 53s. 6½d. 1377: 5 (with Muscott). 1524: 9 (with Muscott). 1674: 17 (with Muscott). *c.* 1720: 12. 1841: 59.

Came in 1625 to Thornton family who built mansion and in 18th cent. removed houses, when creating park, to present site.

BURGHLEY (St Martin's Without, Stamford, and Barnack). 123 TF ?049061. III. U.
1086: 11. 1301: 4. 1674: 1.

In 1390 manor consisted of a messuage, 120a. land, and 1 rood meadow. Bought in 1526 by David Cecil of Stamford, whose grandson Wm, Lord Burghley, built mansion here; this had 70 hearths in 1674. Park extends into three modern parishes: original bounds of Burghley unknown.

CALME (in Clipston. 133 SP 714816). I. U.
1086: 5.

Manor belonged to Bury St Edmunds Abbey in 1086. In 1729 it was "now supposed to be called Comb" (within Clipston).

CASWELL (in Green's Norton). 146 SP 651510. IV. C(1963).
1301: 12. 1316. *c.* 1720: 2.

Like Field Burcote (q.v.), belonged to Green family. In 1509 Sir Nich. Vaux of

Harrowden (who had married Green's heiress) enclosed and converted 300a. to pasture and destroyed 5 houses—apparently whole hamlet. In 1547 Caswell used (with Norton and adjacent hamlets) by John Hickling's flock of 2,000 sheep. Factory on site since 1958.

CATESBY, NETHER. 132 SP 515596.   IV.   C(VS)(1963).
c. 1720: 1.

Nunnery founded temp. Ric. I endowed with whole village. In 1495 prioress destroyed 14 houses and enclosed and converted 16 virgates to pasture, but 5 houses survived at Dissolution. Parish church at Upper Catesby destroyed at Dissolution, and new church built at priory site at Nether Catesby, near mansion. At Nether Catesby hall, farm, and 4 cottages remain. Doubtful whether earthworks are priory alone or village and priory.

CHARWELTON, CHURCH (in Charwelton). 132 SP 545555.   IV.   B(1963).
1316.

This village, also called Great or Lower Charwelton, was taxed with Little or Upper Charwelton. Rous in 1491 reported depopulation of latter (which has since recovered), and warned that Lower Charwelton was "in danger." Most of parish belonged to Biddlesden and Thorney Abbeys, whose lands leased in late 15th cent. by Thos. Andrew; his son kept 1,200 sheep here in 1547. Large pasture owned by Knightley of Fawsley (q.v.) maintained 500 sheep in 1547, while another freeholder had 300. Now only church and one farm.

CHELVERDESCOTE.   I.   U.
1086: 14.

Unidentified manor, mentioned again in 12th cent. survey of county. Perhaps near Everdon Magna.

CHURCHFIELD (in Oundle). 134 TL 013876.   III.   C(1963).
1301: 9.   1316.   1674: 1.   *c.* 1720: 1.

Comprised two manors, one of which came in 15th cent. to Tresham of Sywell. The other, owned by freeholder of Stoke Doyly (adjacent), consisted in 1465 of one messuage and 60a. land. *c.* 1720 "mansion house," with "Chapel Close" adjacent. This perhaps present Wakeley Lodge, where moat visible in 19th cent. Name preserved in modern Churchfield Farm (now within Benefield by boundary change of 1895). Manor excavated by Oundle School *c.* 1960. One farm remains.

COTES or COTEN (in Gretton). 133 SP ?890926.   III.   U.
1316.   *c.* 1720: 1.

Manor consisted in 1290 of one messuage with 70a. arable, 10a. meadow, and rents of £1 0s. 8d. In 1355 described as one messuage, 160a. arable, 20a. meadow, and

20a. pasture. "Cotton Meadow" mentioned in 1569. Several wells near railway may indicate site.

COTTON, MALLOWS (in Raunds and Ringstead). 134 SP 977734. N. A(1964).
Despite absence of taxation and population data, the earthworks at this site indicate a medieval settlement. A manor known as Middlecotes may have been in this village.

COTTON, MILL (in Ringstead). 134 SP 974746. N.   B(P)(1964).
Despite absence of taxation and population data, the earthworks (levelled in 1964) indicated a small medieval settlement which may correspond to a manor of Milne Cotes or Parva Cotes; a third manor, West Cotton or Wylwencotes, has not been located.

DOWNTOWN (in Stanford on Avon). 133 SP 613801. N.   A(P)(1964).
Taxed with Stanford. c. 1720 stated that "large foundation stones and causeys" had been ploughed up. Name perpetuated in Downtown Hill. Site completely deserted.

EAGLETHORP (in Warmington). 134 TL 076917.   IV.   B(HOU)(1956).
Belonged with Warmington to Peterborough Abbey. In 1398 5 free tenants here, possibly with some villeins. Before Dissolution freeholds acquired by Sir Ric. Sapcote of Elton (Hunts.) (adjacent); some copyholds were "decayed" by his son c. 1570. c. 1720 this former hamlet of "about 10 houses" found to be depopulated. Now resettled as suburb of Warmington.

EASTON NESTON. 146 SP 703493.   IV.   D(COV)(1958).
1316.   c. 1720: 1.   1841: 36.
Taxed with Hulcote (which survives). Small park created c. 1500 by Sir Ric. Empson by enclosure of 64a. arable and pasture; he also converted 24a. arable to pasture. Manor bought in 1531 by Ric. Fermor, London merchant. In 1541 manor-house in park, meadow, and pasture mentioned. Only mansion and church remain.

EDGCOTE. 145 SP 505479.   V.   B(1958).
1086: 25.   1301: 31.   1316.   1334: 71s.   1377: 95.   1524: 16.   1674: 19.
c. 1720: c. 18.   1841: 83.
Partial depopulation in 1502, when 120a. arable enclosed and converted to pasture, 120a. pasture enclosed, and 9 houses destroyed. In 1547 500 sheep maintained. Wholly enclosed before c. 1720. Mansion built in village in 1752. Before 1788 village demolished and 2 new farms and 7 cottages rebuilt outside park, leaving church and rectory isolated.

ELKINGTON. 133 SP ?620760. III. C(VS)(1964).

1086: 17. 1316. 1377: 30. 1674: 7. *c.* 1720: 10. 1841: 46.

Whole village and church belonged to Pipewell Abbey. In 1412 stated that pestilence had reduced population to 3 or 4 Pipewell Abbey servitors. Arable all converted before Dissolution, at which time 8 large pastures and grange bought by various county gentlemen. In 1547 sheep totalled 4,000. Only one house survived at Dissolution; most of later farms were 'lodges' built on pastures, and only 3 of houses of 1729 were at the site of the village. Farm cottage and hall remain.

ELMINGTON (in Ashton). 134 TL 055884. IV. U(1963).

1301: 10. 1674: 2. *c.* 1720: 1.

Usually taxed with Oundle in Polebrook Hundred. Two estates in 'Elmington' in 1086, with populations of 9 and 4; both belonged to Crowland Abbey. Both mentioned, but not separately, in 1377. Abbey enclosed and converted 20a. to pasture in 1490, and 160a. between 1494 and 1513, destroying 6 houses and leaving one house and 3 cottages. *c.* 1720 said that foundations of buildings ploughed up within previous 30 years.

ELMINGTON (in Tansor). 134 TL 053909. IV. U(1963).

1301: 11. 1316.

See Elmington (above). This part was usually taxed with Tansor in Willybrook Hundred. *c.* 1720 said to have formerly consisted of 4 or 5 families.

FALCUTT (in Helmdon). 145 SP 595430. V. C(VS)(1958).

1316. 1841: 82.

See Astwell. Called "hamlet" *c.* 1720 but no population stated. Population halved in mid-19th cent. Church and site of manor-house remain, with scattered farms and modern housing away from site.

FAWSLEY. 133 SP 566567. IV. C(1964).

1086: 17. 1301: 44. 1316. 1334: 56s. 8d. 1377: 90. 1524: 7. 1674: 8. *c.* 1720: 6. 1841: 48.

Manor bought by Ric. Knightley in 1415. In 1524 two Knightleys paid subsidy on 100 marks for land and £300 for goods (other payments being for wages). In 1547 2,500 sheep kept here. *c.* 1729 4 houses were "dispersed in the fields." Mansion and church remain in park.

FAXTON (in Lamport). 133 SP 785752. V. A(1958).

1086: 21. 1316. 1334: 38s. 8d. (with Mawsley, q.v.). 1377: 94 (with Mawsley). 1674: 34 (perhaps with Mawsley). *c.* 1720: 32. 1841: 90.

Reduction from 32 houses in 1729 to 15 in 1801 probably connected with enclosure of open fields in 1745. Mansion demolished before 1885. Population nearly doubled by mid-19th cent., but depopulated in early 20th cent. by migration; 11 houses in 1901, all now empty. Church in ruins.

FIELD BURCOTE (in Green's Norton). 146 SP 667508.   IV.   C(1963).
1301: 9.   1316.   1841: 10.
In 14th cent. passed with Green's Norton and Caswell (q.v.) to Green family, law-yers with extensive estates. In 1499 Sir Thos. Green destroyed 4 houses and enclosed and converted 200a. to pasture. In 1551 "lands, meadows, and pastures" here and in adjacent hamlets occupied with Norton by John Hickling's flock of 2,000 sheep. Called "hamlet" c. 1720. Now single farm.

FOSCOTE (in Abthorpe). 146 SP 662473.   IV.   B(VS)(1958).
1301: 10.   1841: 62 (perhaps including outlying farms in Abthorpe).
Probably taxed with Towcester. Arable cultivation by villagers recorded 1373–1420. In 1488 80a. enclosed and 12 persons evicted on one manor by John Ashby. Another manor belonged to Fermor family of Towcester, who were accumulating lands in vicinity. Now 2 farms and 2 cottages.

FOXLEY (in Blakesley). 145 SP 640517.   N(IV).   B(1963).
c. 1720: 4.
Taxed with Cold Higham. De Foxley family held land here from 14th cent. to 1617; in 1547 they kept 400 sheep. Two farms remain.

FURTHO. 146 SP 774430.   IV.   B(1958).
1086: 15.   1316.   c. 1720: 1.   1841: 16.
Taxed with Cosgrave. Owned by de Furtho family from 13th to 17th cents. In 1547 200 sheep maintained. About 1600 Edw. Furtho enclosed and depopulated village, diverting main road and erecting new church. c. 1720 "the remains of a former vil-lage" were visible. Now one farm, dovecote, and church.

GLASSTHORPE (in Flore). 133 SP 663617.   N(IV).   B(1956).
1086: 6.   1301: 14.   1316.   c. 1720: 1.
Taxed with Nobottle in 1377. One manor bought by Spencer of Althorp (q.v.) in 1515. Principal manor, still inhabited in 1371, divided between heiresses in late 15th cent. In 1547 "Classtropp (sic) Pasture" grazed 200 sheep. "Long depopulated" before c. 1720 when only shepherd's house remained. One farm building alone remains.

GLENDON (in Rushton). 133 SP 846814.   IV.   C(COV)(1964).
1086: c. 14.   1316.   1428: below 10.   c. 1720: 2 or 3.   1841: 44.
See Barford. In 1327 10 tenants. In 1514 9 out of 12 houses destroyed. 494a. of arable enclosed and converted to pasture, and 324a. of pasture enclosed by Robt Malory. In 1547 1,500 sheep maintained. Hall remains.

HALE (in Apethorpe). 134 TL *c*.027934. III. U(1963).
1086: 3. 1301: (figure illegible). 1316.
Usually taxed with King's Cliffe. Only 3 tenants in 1304. Depopulated by Black Death: in 1356 advowson worth nothing "because no one dwells nor has dwelt in Hale since the pestilence." *c*. 1720 ruins of houses and signs of "three long streets" visible within Apethorpe Park. Name perpetuated in Halefield Lodge.

HANTONE. I. U.
1086: 18.
Was in Navesland Hundred (later part of Huxloe Hundred), but no site has been identified.

HOTHORPE (in Marston Trussell). 133 SP 667852. V. C(1956).
1086: 1. 1316. 1334: 36s. 4d. 1377: 57. 1729: *c*. 20. 1841: 16.
Was chapelry of Theddingworth (Leics.). Only 4 able-bodied men in 1539. About 1830 John Cook demolished remaining cottages and housed his tenants in Theddingworth; he also created park. Now consists of hall in park, with 2 farms and modern housing away from site.

KINGSTHORPE (in Polebrook). 134 TL 080856. N(IV). B(P)(1963).
Belonged to Thorney Abbey; acquired after Dissolution by Sir Edw. Montagu of Boughton (q.v.). In 1513 abbey enclosed and converted to pasture 6a. and destroyed one house; and *c*. 1600 Montagus carried out some enclosure "in hamlet of Kingsthorpe." Kingsthorpe Fields surveyed 1603. *c*. 1720 found to be depopulated but "hollow places with marks and foundations of a village" still visible. Moat survives, and name perpetuated in Kingsthorpe Lodge.

KIRBY (in Blakesley). 146 SP 636495. IV. B(1958).
1316. *c*. 1720: 1.
Half hide in Blakesley in 1086 (population 2), appearing as 5 virgates in Great Blakesley which, with church, were granted to St John's Hospitallers *c*. 1194, may represent Kirby. Described in 1361 as "1 messuage and 1 carucate in Kirby." In 1487 lessee from Hospitallers destroyed 5 houses and enclosed and converted 300a. to pasture, but possibly not all in Kirby itself. In 1547 pastures in vicinity grazed by 1,000 sheep. Now one farm and out-buildings.

KIRBY (in Gretton). 133 SP 928926. IV. B(1963).
1086: 6. 1316. *c*. 1720: 1.
Perhaps taxed with Deene. Manor with 2 carucates, acquired by Fineshade Priory *c*. 1300, still tenanted at Dissolution. On second manor Sir Robt Lytton enclosed and converted 80a. to pasture in 1495, and destroyed one house; 5 freeholders bought out after 1517. In 1539 10 able-bodied men. Mansion built 1572 on priory

manor; sold to Chris. Hatton, who acquired lay manor and completed enclosure. Three maps of 1584–7 show hall, gardens, church, and several cottages along vestiges of village street. Former houses in close s.w. of mansion remembered *c.* 1720. Mansion now ruined.

KNUSTON (in Irchester). 133 SP 938661.   N(IV).   C(M)(1958).
1086: 12.   1674: 12.   1841: 42.

About 1500 8 houses in "Irchester and Knuston" destroyed and $13\frac{1}{2}$ virgates and 72a. enclosed and converted to pasture by Wm Coope, Anth. Catesby, and Eusebius Isham. One manor acquired in 1542 by Page family, who occupied manor-house in 1674 and may have removed other houses to present site. Second manor perhaps represented in 1624 by "North Hall" with 4 virgates and some closes, possibly at present Chester House. Described as "a hamlet" *c.* 1720.

LILFORD (in Lilford cum Wigsthorpe). 134 TL 030840.   V.   D(M)(COV) (1963).
1301: 31.   1316.   *c.* 1720: 13.   1841: 36.

Normally taxed with Wigsthorpe. Manor had 26 tenants in 1317. Both places together had only 10 able-bodied men in 1529, but had 31 houses by 1674. Mansion built 1635. Houses of Lilford demolished in 1755 and rebuilt in Wigsthorpe by Sir Thos. Powys, who had acquired manor in 1711. Church demolished *c.* 1780; arches re-erected near river as picturesque ruin. Hall remains in park.

LOLHAM (in Maxey). 123 TF 111078.   N(IV).   C(VS)(1962).
1301: 12.   *c.* 1720: 1.

In 1377 taxed with Maxey and Nunton. Six houses and 100a. arable still survived in 1512. After several changes of ownership, manor bought 1681 by FitzWilliam of Milton (q.v.). Now only farm and two cottages.

MAWSLEY (in Loddington). 133 SP *c.* 801768.   IV.   U(1964).
1316.   *c.* 1720: 1 or 2.   1841: 18.

See Faxton. In 1486 "Mawsley Field," possibly then pasture, held by lord of Loddington from lord of Faxton for 2s. rent. Cottage still called "Mawsley" in 1885.

MILTON (in Castor). 134 TL 145995.   V.   C(1963).
1086: 12.   1301: 15.   1674: 5.

Market and fair granted in 1304. Manor-house in ruins in 1366. In 1485 Robt Wittelbury enclosed his pasture. Open fields surviving in 1519 enclosed before 1576. Manor bought 1502 by Wm FitzWilliam, who kept 500 sheep in 1547. Mansion built about then was enlarged 1720; had large deer park. In 1643 Chapel Close was to N.W. of mansion. Only mansion remains.

MUSCOTT (in Norton). 133 SP 625633.   IV.   A(1958).

1316.   1334: 50s.   c. 1720: 3.   1841: 40.

See Brockhall. In 1547 300 sheep grazed Muscott Pasture. Sir John Spencer of
Althorp (q.v.) bought manor with 4 closes of pasture and meadow in 1576, and
"Muscott Pastures" in 1583. One croft has been excavated.

NEWBOLD (in Catesby). 132 SP 517606.   N(IV).   A(1959).

1301: 13 (with Catesby, q.v.).   c. 1720: 3.   1841: 16.

Probably taxed with Catesby in 1524 and 1674. Rated at 7 ploughs in 1220. Part
held by Catesby Priory; it had "Newboldefeld" in 1535, perhaps by then converted
to pasture. A large warren destroyed c. 1700. Only two cottages remain.

NEWBOTTLE. 145 SP 524368.   IV.   B(VS)(1962).

1086: 25.   1301: 23.   1316.   1524: 3.   1841: 19.

Not usually assessed separately. In 1488 300a. enclosed and converted to pasture
and 6 houses destroyed by Hen., Lord Grey. In 1547 Peter Dormer (of Lee Grange,
Bucks.) kept 1,000 sheep here. Now church, hall, dovecote, rectory, and farm.

NEWBOTTLE (in Harrington). 133 SP 776814.   N(IV).   C(1964).

1086: 4.   1316.

In 1377 taxed with Harrington and Thorpe Underwood. Came in 15th cent. to 2
heiresses, probably non-resident. In 1547 300 sheep kept here. In 1583 consisted of
single house. Name perpetuated in Newbottle Bridge towards N. of Harrington
parish, and Newbottle Lodge w. from bridge. Only farm buildings remain.

NEWTON, LITTLE (in Newton). 133 SP 883833.   IV.   C(1964).

1316.   1377: 18.

Sometimes taxed with Oakley Magna. Rated at 4½ ploughs in 1220. In 1499 only
4 families. In 1540's church in Great Newton allowed to decay and Little Newton's
chapel became parish church. Mansion built here by Tresham family, whose enclosure c. 1600 caused riot. c. 1720 found to be depopulated, with foundations of
houses visible in closes by church. Mansion now demolished, but dovecote remains.

NOBOLD (in Clipston). 133 SP 698821.   N(IV).   A(1964).

1316.

Usually taxed with Clipston. Contained 35 virgates in 1284, under three different
owners. Three fields named in 1381; largest manor then still had tenants but in 1459
only 2 houses. Other manors divided during 15th cent. and 280a. came to Ric.
Isham (d. 1492). Lands probably accumulated in 17th cent. by Buswell family of
Clipston. c. 1720 deserted site in 15-acre Old Nobold Close, half a mile w. of Clipston, included banks and hollows of housing, ditches, main street, and fords on
tracks leading to site. Bones dug up in close called Churchyard. Three fields still

known as Nobold Fields. W. suburb of Clipston, called Nobold, then said to have formerly been "Thorp Nobold."

NUNTON (in Maxey). 123 TF 120073.   N(IV).   C(VS)(1962).
1301: 11.   1524: 11.   c. 1720: 4.
Usually taxed with Maxey and Lolham. Now Nunton Hall and two cottages.

ONLEY (in Barby). 132 SP 520715.   N.   A(1955).
c. 1720: 7.   1841: 19.
In 1345 reference made to "tenements in Onle." In 1484 Wm Catesby leased manors of Barby and Onley. In early 17th cent. both manors bought by Giles Isham, whose brother died in 1651 at Onley. c. 1729 described as "a hamlet of 7 shepherds' houses," but map of 1791 shows "Onley Lodges" as 5 scattered farms.

OVERSTONE. 133 SP c.810655.   V.   D(M)(COV)(1963).
1316.   1334: 63s. 4d.   1674: 42.   c. 1720: 33.   1841: 187.
Had 53 tenants in 1398 and 42 in 1520. Drop between 1674 and c. 1720 may be connected with enclosure in 1727. About 1820 John Kipling enlarged park, destroyed mill beside mansion, made lake, and rebuilt church and rectory outside park. Houses rebuilt at present site on main road.

OXENDON, LITTLE (in Great Oxendon). 133 SP 727840.   N(IV).   C(1962).
1334: 32s.   1377: 50.   c. 1720: 1.   1841: 4.
Divided by 1428 between more than 6 persons. By 1467 manor owned by non-resident Boyvile family. Bought in 1515 by Andrew Palmer, who died in 1525 seised of a messuage and 300a. pasture. In 1547 both Oxendons together grazed by flock of 1,000 sheep. Now single farm.

PAPLEY (in Warmington). 134 TL 106891.   IV.   A(1955).
1301: 12.   1316.   c. 1720: 3.
In 1377 taxed with Warmington. Owned in 14th cent. by de Papley family. In 1456 Ric. Papley sold to Wm Brown, a merchant of Stamford, whose daughter Eliz. Elmes (of Lilford, q.v.) enclosed and converted 200a. to pasture in 1499 and destroyed 7 houses. In 1539 Star Chamber case about enclosure. c. 1720 3 shepherds' cottages. Two cottages remain.

PERIO (in Southwick). 134 TL ?040924.   N(III).   C(1963).
1316.
In 1334 taxed with Southwick. Small priory here endowed with 2 mills and some land; it survived into 16th cent. as chantry. Name survives in Perio Mill. In 1779 the road leading s. called "Perry Lane."

PIPEWELL (in Wilbarston and Rushton). 133 SP *c.* 827856. II. U(1963). 1086: 9. 1674: 2. *c.* 1720: 20. 1841: 121.

Monastic site extending into two parishes. West Grange (not now identifiable) built on site of former hamlet. In 1291 court still held at West Grange. Cistercian Abbey founded 1143 has site further east, beside East Grange, on land assarted from woods. By Dissolution abbey had 196a. arable, 55a. meadow, and 443a. pasture; Middle and West Fields at West Grange were part arable, part pasture. In 1547 whole area maintained 800 sheep.

POTCOTE (in Cold Higham). 145 SP 657527. IV. C(1958). 1316.

Manor and most of land came to Green family, of Green's Norton, before 1428. In 1499 Sir Thos. Green destroyed 4 houses and enclosed and converted 304a. to pasture. In 1551 lands here occupied (with Burcote and Caswell, q.v.) by John Hickling's flock of 2,000 sheep. Potcote then had a warren. Two farms in 1841, as now.

PURSTON (in Newbottle and King's Sutton). 145 SP 518395. N(IV). C(1958). 1086: 7. 1301: 16. 1524: 5. 1841: 58. (All with Little Purston.)

In 1086 2 manors, but Bridge's description of "an hamlet, now divided into Great and Little" suggests more recent division. In 1495 Hugh Parsons, Thos. Barker, and Ric. Leek combined to destroy 6 houses and enclose and convert 280a. to pasture. In 1547 600 sheep kept. In 1605 only 2 "trained men." Manor house remains.

SEAWELL (in Blakesley). 146 SP 630525. N(III). C(1963). 1086: 13. 1316. *c.* 1720: 2.

Held in 2 manors; both came in late 14th cent. to non-resident families known later for enclosures elsewhere. Actual occupier probably Foxley family of Foxley, who kept 400 sheep in 1547. In 1841 2 houses. Site N. of Seawell Farm.

SIBBERTON (in Thornhaugh). 134 TL 064998. III. B(1956). 1301: 18. 1377: 13.

Last reference to church 1389. Font said to be in Wansford church and coffins found in field near site. Soon after 1428 manor passed to non-resident heiress. Now single farmhouse.

SILSWORTH (in Watford). 133 SP 617706. N(IV). B(P)(1964). *c.* 1720: 1.

1333 deed refers to hamlet. In 1392 tenements described. Lands much divided between freeholders and 3 monastic houses. One freeholder family accumulated holdings in early 15th cent.; these and other lands, acquired by Wm Catesby of Ashby St Ledgers (adjacent), described in 1485 as 300a. land and 490a. pasture, and in

1594 as 3 "closes or pastures" called Middle Field, High Field, and Sharrock's Close. In 1547 Watford and Silsworth together maintained 2,000 sheep. Silsworth Lodge remains but not at site, where a single cottage stands.

SNORSCOMB (in Everdon). 133 SP 597561. IV. C(1958).
1086: 4. *c.* 1720: 5. 1841: 13.
Smaller manor merged with Everdon; larger manor occupied by Lovel family in 13th and 14th cents.; came to Catesby family in 15th cent. Bought in 1531 by Knightley of Fawsley (q.v.), who was prosecuted for enclosure of 200a. and depopulation of 9 houses here. Now single farm.

STEANE (in Farthinghoe). 145 SP 555390. III. B(1958).
1086: 16. 1301: 16. 1316. 1334: 40s. 4d. 1377: 51. 1428: below 10.
c. 1720: 2. 1841: 26.
By 1428 manor held by Lovel family, with Hinton (adjacent). Forfeited to Crown in 1485; sold later to Thos. Barker, whose son kept 1,000 sheep here in 1547. New chapel built within park *c.* 1620. Manor house, church, and farm remain.

STUCHBURY (in Greatworth). 145 SP 569441. III. A(1958).
1086: 10. 1301: 21. 1316. 1334: 36s. 4d. 1377: 59. 1674: 4. *c.* 1720: 4.
1841: 21.
Belonged to St Andrew's Priory, Northampton. By Dissolution already depopulated; 2 closes called "Westfyld" and "Townefyld" let for £23, and no houses or tenants mentioned. In 1547 Thos. Stuttesbury kept 1,000 sheep on Stuchbury Pastures. Now Hall and farm.

SULBY. 133 SP 653815. III. A(1956).
1086: 13. 1316. 1334: 31s. 1377: 89. 1428: below 10. 1674: 5. *c.* 1720: 2
or 3. 1841: 70.
Manor sold after 1215 to Sulby Abbey (Premonstratensian), founded at Welford *c.* 1155; abbey later bought out some freeholders. At Dissolution 300a. in "Bacheresfeld" close (possibly arable), 58a. meadow, and 880a. pasture in 7 closes, including one called "Old Soulby." Leased by John Hales, gent., then granted to Chris. Hatton, but in 1547 used by Lady Lane for flock of 2,000 sheep. Modern housing is at abbey site; village site deserted.

THORPE LUBENHAM (in Marston Trussell). 133 SP 705866. N(IV). B(1955).
1316. 1334: 12s. 1377: 27. 1674: 1. *c.* 1720: 1. 1841: 11.
Chapelry of Lubenham (Leics.) across River Welland, though situated and assessed in Northants. Not distinguished from Marston Trussell in 1086. Manorial ownership, disputed 1406, apparently passed to non-resident heiresses of Glendon and Newbottle (q.v.). Flock of 600 sheep in 1547. Hall rebuilt outside park.

THRUPP (in Norton). 133 SP c.603652.   IV.   U(1963).
1086: c. 10.   1316.   c. 1720: 1.   1841: 46.

Usually taxed with Norton. Daventry Priory acquired most of land and maintained chapel. Had 2 fields, stretching from Watling Street to w. boundary. Enclosed in 1489 by prior; 400a. converted to pasture, 18 houses destroyed and chapel abandoned. At Dissolution an enclosed pasture called "Thropfeldes." Small lay manor, with only one house in 1564, appears in 1586 in Spencer estate at Althorpe (q.v.) as "Thruptown Field." Modern farms scattered.

TORPEL (in Bainton). 123 TF 113050.   N(III).   C(1962).
1301: 8.

Hamlet of 10 virgates (half in villeinage) in 1276. Market and fair granted in 1264. Manor acquired by Crown in 1280. Castle built in 14th cent. in park. In 1329 253a. arable in demesne and 21 tenants. In 1605 no tenants. In 1547 park maintained 50 cattle.

TRAFFORD (in Chipping Warden). 145 SP 527486.   N(IV).   C(1958).
1086: 6.   1301: 13.   1316.

Usually taxed with Byfield. Manor owned in 13th and 14th cents. by de Trafford family. In 1547 600 sheep kept. Now only Trafford House.

UPTON. 133 SP 717603.   V.   D(COV)(1956).
1086: 20.   1301: 49.   1316.   1334: 72s. 6d. (tenth).   1524: 9.   1674: 13.
c. 1720: 11.   1841: 59.

Drop in population before 1524 perhaps due to acquisition of manor in 1420 by Ric. Knightley of Fawsley (q.v.). c. 1729 mention of some recent enclosure, which may have caused drop in population up to 1801 (4 houses). Now Hall and church in park, and some outlying farms.

WALCOT (in Southorpe). 123 TF 080042.   IV.   D(COV)(1963).
1301: 18.   1377: 40.   1674: 2.   c. 1720: 2.

Perhaps taxed with Barnack. Belonged to Fauvel family in 13th and 14th cents. and in late 15th cent. to Robt Browne (probably of Stamford). Latter family continued till 1661 when heiresses sold manor to Bernard Walcot, who built mansion. Depopulation perhaps connected with non-residence of Brownes. A formerly enclosed warren mentioned c. 1720. Hall and farm remain.

WALTON (in King's Sutton). 145 SP 506346.   IV.   B(1959).
1086: 10.   1301: 17.   1316.   c. 1720: 2.

Usually taxed with Aynho. In 1487 200a. enclosed and converted to pasture and 5 houses destroyed by John Goylyn. In 1506 manor had 10 houses, with 40a. arable, 100a. meadow, and 500a. pasture. In 1537 Ric. Fermor prosecuted for enclosure.

Flock of 1,000 sheep kept here and at King's Sutton in 1547. Chapel Field known to Bridges and chapel ruins seen two hundred years earlier by Leland. Now 2 farms at site.

WOODCROFT (in Etton). 123 TF 138045. N(IV). D(1963).
1301: 35. 1316. 1674: 5.

In 1377 taxed with Etton. Manor divided between heirs in 1434, bought by Fitz-William of Milton in 1530's. In 1547 200 sheep kept on "Woodcroft Pastures." Woodcroft Castle at site is moated mansion with 13th-cent. tower.

WOTHORPE. 123 TF 030056. IV. C(VS)(1963).
1086: 16. 1301: 19. 1377: 40. 1524: 22. 1674: 7. 1841: 68.

Great and Little Wothorpe each had nunnery. That at Gt Wothorpe depopulated by Black Death. At Dissolution whole territory granted to Cecil of Burghley (adjacent). In 1553 Wothorpe still had c. 200a. arable in 3 fields. Mansion built as dower-house for Burghley, now in ruins. Ric. Cecil had advowson of parish church in 1540. Now no church: possibly demolished and village destroyed when Burghley House and Wothorpe House built. Part of Wothorpe parish included in Burghley Park. Area repopulated from Stamford in modern times.

WYTHEMAIL (in Orlingbury). 133 SP 840719. III. A(P)(1954).
1316. c. 1720: 1.

Rated at 6 ploughs in 1220. Chapel mentioned in 1357. In late 15th cent. Wythmale heiress married Sir Thos. Pulteney of Misterton (Leics.). Manor acquired in 1565 by Lord Vaux of Harrowden (adjacent) who also held Badsaddle (q.v.). Park created in 1614 from the common fields of Orlingbury. One house survives. One croft excavated before bulldozing for agriculture in 1954.